The Excuse-less Life

34 Inner-laws For Living Above Distraction

Undrai Fizer

DIVINE HOUSE
B O O K S

ISBN: 978-0-578-16833-3

The Excuse-less Life

34 Inner-laws For Living Above Distraction

Undrai Fizer

ACKNOWLEDGMENT

To my family, friends, and the practitioners of
The Path all over the world!

Table of Contents

INTRO...

When you've been affected by so many disappointments in life, it's possible to reach a point where you'll simply begin to accept them as a "part of life itself." We call it REALITY, or simply, LIFE. And because of this "reality," we find it easy to lean on the side of hopelessness rather than "Creative Thinking or Living!" In order to not be disappointed, we establish a life of no expectations, just to be on the safe side. Where there is no expectation, there is no disappointment. No fulfillment. No adventure. No power. Just a comfort zone called "toil!"

There is a familiar scripture that was written by a king named Solomon that reads, "What has been is what will be, and what has been done is what will be done, and there is nothing new under the sun,"

Ecclesiastes 1:9, English Standard Version. Many of us see LIFE this same way. There is nothing new under the sun. Life is what YOU make it. When we feel this way, we are actually feeling, or even sensing, that there is nothing actually "renewable within us." It's as though Life itself has thrown away the script of our lives and "is holding us captive to the daily routines and rhythms that we've been connected to all of our lives." Excuses have become the new verbiage and mediators of our lives, simply giving us something "new" to say or experience when actually there is really nothing new to experience.

Distractions have become common, exempting us from the Hope we have within our hearts. It's as though we "expected them to be there, on point, and ready to go every time the inspiration to do something different is stirred within us." Nothing new under the sun. Do YOU feel that you'll never experience "anything NEW in YOU, or from YOU?" Maybe, just maybe, NEW is for those who can "afford it!" Do YOU really believe that?

Our Journey in LIFE becomes predictable, boring, and common-place. We are "dying" inwardly, even while we live and vacation. We experience new sunrises every morning "while night constantly resides within the confines of our imagination, spirituality, and relationships." Is this who we really are?

Do YOU actually believe this?

I believe the TIME has come for us to speak something NEW from ourselves. The TIME has arrived to "stir up the Power" that's been lying dormant within us for years. Excuses and Distractions have held us captive for so long that the Beautiful Language of Creativity, Sensitivity, and Divine Life, have fallen victim to slumber, and to actually believe that we can shift atmospheres "seems too silly and surreal to naturally comprehend within our Consciousness!"

Shift Atmospheres?

NOW is the TIME to elevate our mental reality

and break new ground. And no, you're not too old!
Let's not use that as an excuse.

Inner-Law #1

Beauty of The Soul...

Everyday, YOU experience the things that dominate "your attention!" Whatever, or Whoever it is that "owns your attention," will tend to YOU, your mind, and your spirit! It is within YOU to create either "power or pitifulness!" ~The 365

Evolution of the soul will naturally give YOU permission to "embrace the beauty of your life." Deep down, many of us feel ashamed, impoverished, undeserving, and downright ignorant, childish, and stupid. Some of us feel ashamed because WE KNOW that we have not maximized every legitimate opportunity, or relationship, and we feel the sting of that missed connection.

We feel that we may have rushed through our lives and settled for not only the second best thing, but maybe the third, fourth, or fifth best thing down the line. We are ashamed because we have wasted our time, and we are constantly reminded that the TIME isn't coming back. We are ashamed because we feel ignorant and we are constantly surrounded by individuals who always seem to ask us something in the genre of what we have yet to commit ourselves to know. We give answers that we are not comfortable with, fearing that someone will see through those answers and find out that we are frauds to our own selves.

We feel that we must constantly be told what to do, how to do, what to think, how to think, where to go, and why to go! Are you going to ever grow up? We feel childish and sad, mainly because we know that we have done this to ourselves. Everyone knows where they have "tailored made" much of their life's course, simply out of fear of discipline, settled-ness, and discernment.

How do YOU view your life NOW? Have YOU, given YOU, everything YOU deserve? Have YOU determined what YOU deserve? No one is required to give YOU what YOU deserve. Many will give us what they think we deserve, but those choices are determined by their own evaluation. Have YOU granted yourself what YOU deserve, based on your own evaluation? Have YOU determined that YOU weren't significant enough, so you decided not to burden Destiny out of fear of wasting its Time?

: : A LIVING LAW: :

I remember feeling this way myself. Everyone's perspective of confidence is different, but I remember when this thing SHIFTED for me and remained. I'm not one for formulas, but SHIFTS are awakened when YOU unlock the first piece of the Inner Mystery of YOU. **ALLOWANCE** is the first key to the unfamiliar. Try ALLOWING yourself the power, and capacity, to be the "center of Attention" for Change and Difference. Try "letting" yourself BE the attention of Wisdom, Correction, and Discipline. Stop giving other things the attention that YOU should be granting yourself. It feels funny when YOU haven't practiced this reality on yourself. Practice this over and over again. Try doing this while "resisting the temptation of guilt, and false feelings of arrogance," just for the fact that you're thinking about yourself. When YOU begin to ALLOW yourself to BE the center of attention for change, A SHIFT will "tap YOU on the shoulder!"

Inner-Law #2

Becoming ME!

"When you're in love with The Path, the walk will naturally reveal itself to YOU." ~ The 365

I'm constantly living, breathing, and flowing in myself. I take breaks without "disrupting my flow of LIFE!" I rest without resting. I stop without ending. I no longer give energy to trivial things. I'm BEING me in a beautiful way. I have POWER, simply because I no longer "need power," over anyone else. I needed power to handle my feelings when I felt violated, or defenseless, when my life's choices were questioned. I needed something to help me "handle my feelings" when my weakness was exposed. I needed something to help me handle my feelings when my "darkness" was exposed. I needed something to help me handle my feelings when my ignorance was exposed. I needed something to help me handle my feelings when my heart was exposed. I felt that I needed POWER.

But the truth of the matter is that I needed "to accept" my Path. I needed to know IF I was actually living a Path. I hadn't accepted all of ME. I accepted what I wished my LIFE could be, but I hadn't accepted ME. I accepted what I wished my life would create, but I hadn't accepted me. I accepted what someone else told me that I could be, but I hadn't accepted ME. I had yet to accept my darkness. I needed to accept my darkness before I could open my eyes to my LIGHT. I had yet to accept my everything.

I needed to be the one to make sense of "my two sense!" I needed to be the one to comprehend my wisdom. I wasted so much time trying to get others to "get me" when I had not yet "received myself!" I wanted to be a gift to the world "when I had yet to accept my own present of SELF!" I cannot expect others to receive me "when I was constantly throwing myself away!"

I wanted others to treat me with the respect that I despised giving myself. I was corrupting my world instead of blessing my world. The more evolution stirs "the More I see that I am becoming ME!"

: : A LIVING LAW: :

It took me awhile, but I didn't know that it was an intricate part of the Evolutionary Process of Spirit. I didn't think, or even imagine, that I was a very interesting individual. I didn't think that anything, or anyone, was interested in me. I had no positive interest in ME. In order to awaken the Power of Positive, and the Vibe of Love around YOU, it is imperative to find an interest in yourself. Say it to yourself, *"I AM Interesting!"* When we innately feel "ugly" within, we give permission to the Atmosphere to ignore our existence. This is why we feel "disconnected, unheard, or matter–less!" Say to yourself, *"I AM Interesting!"* Begin to speak out your own name. Begin to love the sound of your name. Begin to give an impromptu interview to Yourself. When I feel that I'm not interesting, I will grant permission to Excuse and Distraction to do its bidding with me.

INNER-LAW #3

BEFRIENDING YOUR TIME...

Within YOU are all the people YOU need to get it done!" ~The 365

I cannot get lost with time when I AM a friend of my time. LIFE, and TIME, will treat YOU according to the degree YOU live it. Most people live life with a certain reality. Many are not usually drawn to things that they consider "deeply spiritual, or wordy!" Many simply see the Human Experience as a combination of decisions and choices, with a hint of good and bad events thrown in for flavor. The "deep things" are for those who may be escaping the reality of life, so they "create another life through imagination!"

This may be true for some in most cases. There are those who seek to escape the responsibilities of Life by creating some sort of "irresponsible reality or playground" in order to cope with life's continual demand upon their potential! But I have found that when purposely elevating your personal realm of consciousness, awareness, and spirit, a renewed frequency of energy, potential, and consistency will awaken within YOU. You will find yourself living empowered and fulfilled!

Have YOU befriended your TIME? I AM at peace with my TIME. Goals are the reflections and offspring of those who have become best friends with their MOMENTS. Every moment is special. Every moment awaits a signature from me in order to do my bidding. I AM a friend of my TIME and a "parent of my moments!" TIME is "an invisible servant that awaits a command from your LIFE!" TIME isn't waiting for YOU to die. No, TIME is waiting to LIVE from your command!

Excuses and Distractions are natural responses to the LIFE that has no friendship with TIME. Nurture your relationship with TIME by communicating with it through your life's work and vision. Live an "elevated lifestyle" through your Spirit and Desire. Never allow yourself to become so domesticated that YOU lose your own worth of Self and Spirit. Excuses will become your friend "when you lose faith and significance in your own Self!" Excuses and Distractions will not allow YOU to "set yourself free in Mind!" When you become free "where will the Excuses and Distractions go?"

Befriend your time by befriending **yourself.** Go ahead and say it, *"I AM my friend!"* **When you** are a friend to your TIME *"it will take YOU to new places in your soul and also in your LIFE!"* **Wh**en you are a friend to your TIME "a **feeling of LOVE** will overwhelm YOU, and you wi**ll find that LI**FE actually desires to hear from YOU!"

: : A LIVING LAW: :

Truth becomes physical and tangib**le the Mom**ent "YOU begin to feel the way Truth **feels!" I had** to rid myself of the domestic and hum**anistic reason**ing of Logic, before my Imagination an**d Truth beca**me a tangible reality in my LIFE. Defi**ne the Truth t**hat YOU are passionate in living. You'**re going to h**ave to allow the "crazy and absurd" vi**sion to beco**me the Wisdom of your life. I had to c**hoose the re**alm of Spirit that I wanted to live the **rest of life fr**om. This realm of Spirit would be to**tally responsi**ble for my perspectives, feelings, and **understandi**ng. I knew that I would be misundersto**od by many**; but it was a choice I was willing to make. It feels like magic, but believe me, "it's far from magic!" YOU must be willing to allow this Wisdom total access to your life.

The more I kept flowing in this passion of my LIFE, I began to experience the qualities of what I call, "The Divine Mind." I wasn't feeling more "sanctified, or morally perfect!" I began to experience a "different type of Sacredness" that made me feel more assured in where I lived within ME. There is an intellectual surety, and then there is a spiritual surety. Not one of religious awareness, but of Personal Awareness. It was at this point that I was no longer "renting myself to others to be abused!" From this mentality, or Consciousness, I began to feel like "the lord" that I was created to be, and I felt an authority that gave me the right to bless TIME with my ideas and existence.

INNER-LAW #4

COMFORT IN MY SKIN...

"Confidence confirms that intimidation is absent from the soul," ~The 365

A m I growing more comfortable within myself in my own skin? Am I appreciating myself, loving myself, and seeing myself evolving even more into a greater essence of the Divine BEING that I already am? As a matter of fact, while I'm asking myself all of these questions, what is this "Divine BEING" thing anyway? You know, since I'm asking questions and all.

Sometimes, our greatest answers come through "the constant inner questioning of the soul." Questions are merely "hidden answers that seek the Light of a response!" The purest essence of possessing LIGHT is not always found in how "good" we are being, but in how comfortable we are becoming in our authentic self. The common notion that many obligate themselves to when it comes to God, the Divine, or Truth, is "how good are we becoming?" instead of how "true" are we becoming? How true ARE WE becoming?

As a teacher and facilitator of what I call "The Path," it was imperative for me to see how well my associates and sharers of this Divine LIFE, were growing within themselves. Not necessarily growth to see how "sinless" they were becoming, but how "excuseless" they were becoming. I wanted to know how comfortable they were becoming "in their own skin, their own thoughts, and their own perspectives of where they were in this LIFE called THE PATH, or The WAY." I wanted to know how comfortable they were in the darkness, as well as the Light. They needed to become powerfully intimate in the realm of their own discernment and sight. I wanted to know if my life "was inspiring them" to "see in themselves," the same DIVINE Reality that they saw in me.

Growth should never be considered in the magnitude of the audience to which a teacher presents themselves, but in the magnitude of the DIVINE that the listener, or sharer, "can see within themselves" without shame, burden, or limitation. Can I SEE THE GOOD in myself, without feeling ashamed about it? Can I see the beauty of my life without feeling that I'm going to lose it if I recognize it?

: : A LIVING LAW : :

I remember when I lived with my grandparents
in Heflin, Louisiana when I was a little boy.
My grandmother was the *"most sweetest and
beautifullest"* woman I'd ever known, as I'm sure
your grandmother was to YOU also! She was
a world traveler and would bring me books and
souvenirs from Jerusalem and Rome during her
Holy Land trips.

Well, I can't tell YOU when I got "this feeling"
within me. But as long as I can remember, I felt
like I was a *"divine individual,"* or some *"son of God!"*
My usual playtime consisted of being characters
named Jesus, or either Moses. I would play with my
cousins in the fields that my grandparents owned
and I would lead them "out of Egypt" as we played.
No one told me to do it. I just "felt it" in me. I
remember getting those old, Kerr jars and filling
them up with water, and sitting alone in the field,
having conversations with God. I use to hear His
Voice within me. I already felt like I was some sort

of *"god,"* even as a little boy. No outside coercion, teaching or instruction. It was simply love and *a child-like* connectivity to the greatest possibility that I've ever known! From this inner-law, my creativity in life, music, and understanding, found its way to the LIGHT! What I AM saying to YOU is this; *Embrace your WAY*, no matter how unique and unfamiliar it may be to others. When YOU haven't embraced your *"Way,"* YOU will find yourself being led into "realms of motion" that do not belong to YOU!

Embrace your unique, and divine "way!" The Confidence will come when YOU refrain from giving other people the power to make it "right, or wrong!"

Inner-Law #5

Communion with Self...

Whatever is yours, will call out to YOU daily!
Sometimes, Purpose isn't found in what YOU see
yourself doing, but in what YOU see yourself answering!
~The 365

Every Moment is a reality of Prayer to Me. I am constantly talking to myself. If I AM who God is, then every time I think to myself, I am communing with God. I see God no different from me. I do not see God *standing apart* from Me. I feel that I am *interwoven within every fiber of the Divine Life*. I am not separated from it, neither am I "standing apart" from it. I am totally interfused with the very essence of everything DIVINE. As I speak to myself, "I speak within the soul of God!"

I am communing with the Voice of the Divine in every way. My thoughts. My feelings. My work. My daily rhythm and life flow, communes with God. Even when I'm angry, I am speaking to God. Even when my thoughts are not on God, "they are on God!" God is everything. Everything is everything. There is nothing that I can think of God, that He is NOT! Is this what it's like to be "the temple of God?" Maybe so.

Your life is how you permit yourself to see it. You may not see your life this way. You may think it's crazy for me to say this. I feel this Openness to the Divine in every moment. I feel like "I'm in" all of the time. I am never "out" of God. I am always "in" the rhythm of the Never Ending Essence of the Divine at all times. I'm settled in it. Even during those times where I act "foolish, mannish, or playful," I find myself never feeling disconnected from the Divine. You can't leave something that takes up the space of everything. God is ALL. Where can you go? You can't leave if you tried. Well, unless you "permit" yourself to be disconnected "in mind" and in your sense of Self.

I can't leave. Where can I go "where the Divine isn't already occupying?" Since there is no place for either of us to go, we remain interwoven within each other. As I speak to myself, even as I speak to YOU, I am speaking with God. Because our lives are prayers, we experience incredible and powerful "intuitions!" When we live from The Path, our "inner flow" perceives goodness, love, possibilities, and power. When we live from fear, we perceive pain, misery, and deceit! It's all intuition. But the nature of the Path we live from "will determine the type of fruition we experience from intuition!"

Is this what we call "prayer life?" Prayer life is not the moment in which YOU pray, but in the never ending rhythm and continual evolution in your communion to your Divine Self.

: : A LIVING LAW: :

When I put an end to condemning myself, I stopped doing "condemnable things!" When I stopped being fearful, I put an end to "listening out for fear!" When I put an end to "listening for chaos," I began to hear LIGHT! I began to constantly hear LIGHT from me, through me, and to me! I overcame the inner fear of being "like God!" I didn't seek to be perfect. I sought to live the thought that God had of me when I was created. I became a person that couldn't be condemned. I became brutally honest with myself, and my "insecurities!" I began to question myself and say, "What can anyone do to me?" The answer would always come back to "fear, doubt, and unbelief!" When you are easily offended, you are easily distracted!

I allowed myself to be powerful and important. I didn't set a limit on how significant, or important, to feel. I simply felt. I granted myself every permission available, and may have even created permissions without the consideration of others. All I know is that when YOU are afraid of becoming intimate with the knowledge and wisdom of your own spirit and purpose, YOU will not awaken the Power to escape Distractions, Fears, or Excuses. These "evil things" are the rhetoric for those who are yet blind.

YOU too are free to do the same…

"Diamonds and Treasures!"

*"When you are inspired by some great
purpose, some extraordinary project, all your thoughts
break their bonds: Your mind transcends limitations,
your consciousness expands in every direction, and you
find yourself in a new, great, and wonderful world."*
~Patanjali

My Path is like a diamond that fell down the drain. The value and loveliness of this precious object naturally inspires me to extend my fingers through the entrance of the drain, to "see" if I can reach it, or touch it. When I see that it doesn't work, I seek for a wire hanger, or any elongated contraption, to at least "show an attempt" to retrieve my precious commodity! When all else fails, I call a plumber, whom I know possesses the tools that are able to open the pipe, so I can retrieve my treasure!

Purpose is a gift that reveals the treasures of your soul, as well as the preciousness of your time. It will naturally "reinvent your disciplines, persona, and perspective." The value of the treasures of YOU, will naturally reshape and re-design, the perceptions of thought that were responsible for "forming you into the image that you are evicting yourself from" at this moment. You will soon find excuses leaving your life as well.

What is "your" diamond? What is "your" treasure of mind and spirit? For a treasure "we will change our own worlds and galaxies of Thought and Life!" We will never change for something that is a treasure in someone else's eyes. It's close to impossible to find value in a thing that is only valuable to someone else. It must become a value and a treasure to US first. For our own diamonds, we shift! For our own treasures, we transform!

Our habits and disciplines become as new as the "tools we seek" in order to retrieve the treasures that have fallen down the drain! Behaviors will shift when it has found a treasure that is greater than the habits we already possess! When YOU discover the Beauty of Your Existence, a shift will happen quickly, aggressively, and naturally! No "step by step" coaching is required. When you've discovered the treasure of life, your life will attract a transformation, not mere modification!

What is your diamond? What is your treasure? I cannot pursue what isn't pursuing me. Excuses will constantly lend their protection to me when "pursuing things that aren't pursuing me!"

Obligation does not establish commitment within me. It creates failure and limitation. It establishes the need to "lie," or give the permission to excuses to speak on my behalf!

: : A LIVING LAW: :

I actually feel that my ideas, and sparks of the soul, are real treasures. I believe that my ideas can support me and my lifetime. I believe that my family and friends can benefit from them. I believe the world can benefit from them. Regardless of what I receive financially from my ideas, I believe that I AM wealthy. TRUST is a hard word for most. I trust my Thoughts. I have "evolved" from simply "believing it." I trust it. I have given myself to my LIFE. I remember my early years of marriage with Bridget. We were being evicted from the first apartment we ever had as a newly married couple. I remember being mentally "shocked" at the happenings of that day. I had grown accustomed to God "saving the day" for me. But in this particular moment, a Shift had occurred, and I wasn't told about it. As they were taking our possessions and throwing them in the truck, Bridget and I drove away, not knowing what to do. I was also afraid of being perceived as a "sorry husband who didn't have what it took to take care his wife!" I was already feeling the pressure of being connected to people who didn't yet "know me, or my Path in LIFE!" I was living, and pretending, at the same time. I hadn't yet "emotionally" embraced myself fully. I had given other people that right, as well as the power to judge me according to what they saw me to be. Well, after going to the storage where our belongings were being held, we sought to regain those things we lost during the eviction. To our surprise, the storage owners had completely reneged on the agreement that led to our going there in the first place. At this point, there was no way for us to purchase our belongings. So, we had to make a decision. In one of those boxes was information concerning our Vision, Life's Work, and Writings. Believing that our Vision would be the catalyst for "inspiring our comeback," we left about 95 percent of what we owned. We retrieved the papers, and a few incidentals, and left, putting total trust in our Purpose and Destiny! YOU will have to decide what's important for YOU, as well as your LIFE! I did what I felt was not only important, but critical for my life, destiny, and purpose! I see myself as "the Diamond!"

I trust it.

DRIFTING EVEN FURTHER

"The new thing that YOU keep saying you're going to be, will do everything it can to make sure that your comfort zones stop liking YOU, in hopes for securing your release!" ~The 365

I'm settled in this deep place. **I'm no longer** expending energies that seek **confirmation** of where I am, why I am, or if I am. **I'm in the** right place. The absence of "chaos" is **no longer** my "confirmation, or sign of agreement," that comes to settle the anxieties within me when encountering an unfamiliar place. I've actually welcomed the "chaos and the unfamiliar." I have accepted it as one of the necessary "pleasures" that accompany this "vast ocean of Oneness!"

I remember when my life was finding itself "drifting even further" into this "darkness of Light!" I remember saying to myself, "I'm out here now!" I was spiritually curious, eagerly anticipating the arrival of bold, new worlds that I previously thought were "out there," but was rather uncomfortably, and surprisingly, discovering were already residing "within Me!" As my spirit ventured even more into this reality, I began to accept the fact that "no one was going to be able to rescue me from where I was headed!" I had reached the point of no return.

No return to the familiar, or the "peaceful." I am truly amazed at this finding. When the "seed of anxiety" finds a "silent residence" within you, it will pervert, and make imperfect, "all of your discoveries." It will never allow you to experience the pleasures of BECOMING. It will grant you the "funds" to "wander in Spirit" without ever allowing you to "seal the deal" with your Life and Self. It will hinder you from experiencing the "security of Thought" which will in turn, secure your decisions.

I live where I need to. I live where I find JOY! I do not consider my Path to be dangerous, or different. It's where my JOY is. I have seized the place of my passion. If my passion seems to be "far away" to you, it's because it wasn't meant to be seized by you! I ventured out to become one with the greatest sound that I've ever heard within me. I've gone to the depths of my soul and made a place called HOME!

I've travelled far away in order to get "closer to myself!" I've journeyed as far as the "disconnection within myself," to the Place where I could reconnect with myself. The Journey to YOU is as long as the "distance you lived apart from YOU!" What is considered "deep" is the impoverishment from which we've sincerely existed within ourselves.

I've gone. I live far away from what was once so familiar. It was familiar but it wasn't family. I knew things about Me that wasn't me. I learned things that did not give me intelligence. I've mastered things of no mastery. I've known things that could not know me. Such poverty. Such waste. I've invested countless hours into a world that couldn't remain alive without my participation in it.

I've travelled an incredible journey.

To me.

: : A LIVING LAW: :

During this Journey of Evolution and Discovery,

my family and I moved to California to live for 3 ½ years. Believe it or not, we left on this Journey with $500 in cash, and a credit card that one of our dear friends allowed us to use on the trip. We had no home prepared for us in California. We left Houston, Texas inspired by a Word, and a Thought. Various events around us "confirmed," or "brought some sanity," to the Inspiration that we felt within our hearts. Well, for 3 1/2 years, we lived in various extended stays, hotels, motels, and temporary rent homes. We became a part of the California culture and its ways. My children loved it and began their public schooling there after being homeschooled since they were very young. During our stay, there were moments of confusion, silence, and wondering. To go so far to live "where no physical person sent an invitation, or promised support for you" while YOU "figure everything out!" The Journey to Discovery can feel like this in your Spirit. Taking giant steps of faith, or even small steps of "I Wonder," can get YOU in the gut at times. YOU must allow yourself to be sure. YOU must know what you're going after and why. Little did I know, the Journey into the Unfamiliar would serve as the catalyst for preparing my Consciousness for a new world within me. Every day, the disciplines of the Unfamiliar would train me, speak to me, and shift me, into an individual that I didn't even know I was. Sometimes, YOU will feel like YOU don't know what you're doing. At these times, look within and ask yourself the Questions you are afraid to ask!

"What AM I doing?" Maybe, YOU just need to sit there and listen...

INNER-LAW #8

EMBRACING THE PATH!!

Half of our mistakes in life arises from "feeling" where we ought to think, and "thinking" where we ought to feel! ~John Churton Collins

---

When I embrace the Path, I will stop perceiving myself as "standing apart" from the Path. I am The PATH. You are THE PATH. I AM where I'm going. There is no such thing as "deep" now. I AM where I'm going, even when I have yet to get there. I AM there, and on my way at the same time. I don't see myself ending, dying, or being done away with. I AM where I'm going.

I AM heaven. I AM a kingdom of beauty and power. I AM fearless. I AM everything I'm supposed to be. I AM here. To live this way is to BE this way. As I become ravishingly courageous in my Authenticity, as well as fearless in my commitment, to both what is LIGHT and what is DARKNESS in my Path, I find myself naturally becoming what THE PATH is all about. I don't have to dictate what I WILL BE. I simply BE. I AM, YOU ARE, the reflection of THE PATH. I AM what the PATH sees within itself. Behavior is the reflection of inner-sight and self-perception. I AM what I see. What I SEE, I AM. Behavior is the essence of how Self is perceived by Self.

If I am ashamed of who I see in Me, my BEHAVIOR will befriend excuse. When I love who I see in Me, my Behavior will seek to "court me, love me, and expose me" to the world called LIGHT! Behavior is the self-created rhythm of Reflection. However YOU see YOU, YOU WILL ACT.

I AM not ashamed to be God. I AM not ashamed to be LIGHT, and darkness. I AM not ashamed to be God, while yet having a "questionable or unfamiliar" reflective within me. I am getting to know what I already know as me. And in my journey, I find myself not afraid. To be God.

Sin is not an action. It is the discomfort in being yourself. It is the discomfort in being the reflection of LIGHT, and even the "Dark." It is the discomfort in living your beauty. Sin is the shamefulness in being yourself, and the proudness in being another!

: : A LIVING LAW: :

Certain people would get offended when I would say, *"I AM, not afraid to be God!"* No, I AM not the Creator of the Universe. As I continued on the beautiful Path of "unfolding and unwrapping myself," I began to find an even more, spiritual pleasure in my I AM-ness with God. I embraced, with confidence, my relationship with Wisdom. The more I spoke of Wisdom, in the form of a Person, the more I began to feel it, see it, and BE it! It was no longer an intellectual reality to me. It was now a LIGHT of LIFE to me. I no longer needed to go to certain places to be "recognized, validated, or approved!" I naturally stopped wasting time looking for events to validate me. Wasting time is distraction on so many levels. When I found myself, I stopped seeking people who could validate me, or approve me. I am a living offspring of Divine Nature. I AM, "what the Nature is." When you are afraid of BEING who you are naturally, TIME won't be what it naturally is, to YOU. You have to determine "what YOU will allow yourself to BE, to YOU!"

Say it to yourself. *"I AM, as God." "I AM, who God is."* Practice your divine identity and reality.

Your ways of LIFE, will always imitate "who YOU feel You are!" Things no longer became "mere information to me." Just a way of LIFE...

Inner-Law #9

Excuses, Excuses...

But Moses said to the Lord, "Oh, my Lord, I am not eloquent, either in the past or since you have spoken to your servant, but I am slow of speech and of tongue."
Exodus 4:10

"I have awesome ideas. Great ideas. Do I need to share them with someone else? What if they don't like them?"

"What is "that look" on their faces?"

"Why don't I feel virtue from them?"

"Is something wrong with my vision?"

"Why are they "hating" on me?"

"Why are they rejecting me?"

"Are they rejecting me?"

"Where did this idea come from anyway?"

"People won't let you have anything of value. People are envious when it's You who's getting the great ideas."

"I guess they don't think that I can do it."

"I'm not their favorite."

'I'm not the person that they see as important. I'm not smart enough."

"I bet if I was on television they would listen to me."

"What's wrong with my idea?"

"Why are they so quiet?"

"What's with "that look?"

"I'm Black!"

"I'm White!"

"I'm a Man!"

"I'm a Woman!"

"I'm divorced!"

"They're prejudiced!"

"I don't have enough money!"

"There's not enough time!"

Alright, you have a vision. What did YOU expect THEM to do when YOU told them?

NOW, what do YOU expect to do with it, since it was YOU who knew it way before "they" did? Are YOU the Person of your own dreams? Do your dreams like YOU? They must like YOU "if they're leaving their belongings in your Mind!"

The motives concerning your ideas will determine your patience, disciplines, and consistency! Why are YOU doing what you're doing? Who told YOU to do it? What problems will it solve? What will it bring to YOU? Motives determine if excuses "will be necessary in your life or not!" Who are YOU trying to impress? Motives will also determine if the Power of Creativity will be consistently stirred within YOU. When your Motives are true, so will your momentum. How much Truth can YOU handle?

Your motives will determine if excuses are befriending YOU, or running away from YOU. YOU will give up the options that will cause LIFE to feel "safe and friendly!"

So, what's your excuse?

: : A LIVING LAW: :

Sometimes, "works of vision" are created from minds that are intimately associated with pain, woundedness, fears of rejection, and the need to be affirmed. Psychologically, a depressed individual can create the most beautiful picture of life, "without factoring in the transformational shift that is required to manifest "this Picture" in the Light! Wounded people can create beautiful conversation that lacks the "wealth of confidence" that will bring the Words to LIFE and create what we call, **LANGUAGE**! When we reveal our ideas, without being whole in Mind and Consciousness, we will naturally expose our "flaws, excuses, and distractions." It will be everyone else's fault on why we didn't produce the Vision. When we are wounded, we somehow "become gifted with x-ray vision!" We usually project in others "the pain, questions, and terror" that is already existing within our own hearts. We are actually feeling this way about our own selves. When we are in pain, we will create a "false light of perfection" that doesn't even have strength enough to shine on us for our own use! VISION comes to transform the Consciousness of "the weak" before it sheds LIGHT on the rest of world. When we are not emotionally whole, your idea may take years before the "motive" that is actually responsible for the idea, has been evicted from the soul, or has died! When we are not emotionally whole, we will consistently, and without hindrance, attract an event that will awaken within us, the most creative excuses known to man!

Inner-Law #10

Forget Everyone Else...

Conformity is the jailer of freedom and the enemy of growth. ~JFK

What is good for me?

What is evil?

What is "wrong?"

What is "sin?"

Am I still obligated to view my life from a book? Who am I? Am I yet trying to coexist with evil? Sin? Lust? Am I trying to create a world in which "I am the king?" Is there no law in my world? No boundaries? Am I making myself into my own god with my own laws? Am I creating a world into my own image and likeness? Am I threatened when others have found shame within it? Who am I trying to be?

What does my life look like without belief in anything? Does my behavior reflect God or goodness? Is Goodness pleased with me? How do I know? Does Blessings of material substance prove that God is pleased with me? Am I comfortable in myself? Am I a bad person? Am I in a conflict with good and evil? Am I in a conflict with the bible? Am I picking and choosing what I want to receive from the bible? Am I following my heart? Am I wicked? Am I blind?

Does having a desire to see people "saved" prove that I love God? Or, is becoming comfortable in my authenticity, while "saving" myself from the fear of being, the "proof" that I love God? Do I want people saved from the discomfort of being? Or, do I want them to stop doing bad things? Why am I angry when I tell them to stop doing bad things "and they yet continue in doing bad things?" Is it because I still want to do bad things and I was told to stop "if I didn't want to go to hell?" Why do I get mad when no one does what I told them to do? Am I threatened by their authenticity? Have I found significance in my ME-SHIP? Am I threatened by their "lord-ship" of Self? Am I afraid to be me, "even if my ME is questionable?"

Have I recognized the salvation of ME? AM I being

saved to recognize an *I AM* within me? Why is my salvation ruining my happiness and my joy? Is it supposed to ruin it? Is my life supposed to lose all sense of fun? Is Awareness "crippling?" Am I supposed to be this angry? Am I supposed to be this sad?

Am I angry because I have to "grow up?" Am I angry because I yet want to employ excuses? Am I angry because I see LIGHT?

: : A LIVING LAW: :

One thing I know is that when YOU actually love the Path you're on, you will give up your power of resistance. YOU may experience moments when YOU need understanding. But it is possible to find yourself in a place of "indecision," while being free of resistance, at the same time. Resistance creates the "inner fighting" that renders us "blind, and unaware, of who we are, as well as where we are, in LIFE!" Your LOVE for the Path, will cause the enemies of your own mind, to become friends with YOU! In our various treks back and forth to California from Texas, we had to learn to give up resistance to the Unfamiliar. As long as we demanded answers from a "Place that had no answers," we would find ourselves disappointed, angry, and confused! When there are others in your life that are requiring answers from YOU, you will find yourself trying to get answers from a "Place that has no answers," and your depression will rise! Maybe, just maybe, the issue is not with "the Place that has no answers," but with the people who are yet in your life, who should not really be in your business at all! When YOU stop being resistant to the Path, YOU will find yourself allowing "the lives that should have left your life a long time ago, a much needed fare-well!" When we are resisting The Passion and The Purpose, "excuses and distractions will find peace with us!" And when things find peace with us, they will have no desire to leave!

INNER-LAW #11

"GOD SHOWS UP WHEN WE DO!"

Torment is when YOU know more than you're willing to do. The Miraculous is when you've done more "than You've ever known!" ~ The 365

The miracles of God are awakened "as soon as I realize the Infinite Truth of myself!" My life will experience chaos when I AM "disconnected from the Light of Myself!" The chaos is a reflection of the disturbance that I have become intimately connected to from within, as a result of my "misperception of the DIVINE LIGHT" that already resided within me.

When my mind is "blind," God too, becomes "blind!" Isn't it funny that God shows up "when YOU do?" When I show up "so does the Divine!" All of the issues of life "are within us." There is really nothing going on "on the outside of us!" It is how we perceive what is around us that creates the issues within us!

There is a Divine Reality that "almost seems too good, too surreal, to be true!" I've given myself to the "uncertainty of the Divine," the "unseen and the unfamiliar dimensions of Imagination," and have allowed this Path to "use me as a vessel!" I've given my very own skin to these incredible Depths of Unfamiliar Wisdom.

Allow yourself to become the Body of the Thought and the Wisdom! Have You given your body to Divine Wisdom?

When will YOU arrive to your Divine Consciousness? Many deem this as some sort of moral perfection. Many have yet to embrace the fact that this "particular perfection" is only found in the settled-ness and comforts of our Divine Identity. Embracing our "god-ness" without question. Embracing it so that it now becomes "impossible to encounter, or even entertain, ANY OPPOSING THOUGHT or IMAGINATION concerning it." When I am settled in ME, *every other voice will either die or refrain from even being born!"*

I AM, without question from myself, or any other entity, a perfect expression of the Being-ness and Thoughtfulness of the Divine. As I live from this perfect reality, it is within me to "shape my world and my doings" for the maximization of my greater essence and responsibility. God arrives "**when I** do!" God is revealed "when I AM reveal**ed to myself!**"

I AM a miracle. I AM a survivor **from the torm**ent that I allowed myself to expe**rience through** ignorance, shame, and unbelief. I **AM a champi**on, as a result of being raised from **the "dead of** my own, self –imposed excuse."

No more…

:: A LIVING LAW: :

I see that many of us are really **affected by** the opinions of others, especially when **it relates to** our own *BEING-ness* and ways of thou**ght! Our "f**ear," of the opinions of those who fin**d their iden**tity and trust "in religion," has had a pr**ofound effect** on how we think, imagine, and perce**ive ourselves.** We will only go as far "as the opinion **allows us to g**o!" Your boldness in life is a complete **reflection of** the core values that YOU hold true **for yourself.** No one can teach YOU boldness. Boldness is a natural offspring of Truth that you've grown intimate with. Excuses and Distractions cannot feed off of someone who has shown a non-compromising, boldness of conviction, within themselves. There are some things you're going to have to become convinced of yourself. Conviction is not taught. It is embraced and established within the heart of the Lover! If you're simply "riding the coattails" of a Wisdom that you are not trusting, the Chaos that you are experiencing is not from an enemy, but from your own dis-trust in Wisdom.

There is a Passion that YOU will discover within YOU. It will serve as an "under-current" within your heart and soul. From "this" Passion, your decisions will be established and carried out. It will seize LIFE, "and take from LIFE," that Part which belongs to YOU and your Lifetime! Distractions come when YOU have yet to "figure out your lane!" This Passion will naturally regulate your existence and articulate it through the form of a story, a creativity, or a sound. It is a highly disciplined, yet flexible reality, of Consciousness! And from this reality, YOU will see God.

So powerfully. So beautifully. So amazingly...

INNER-LAW #12

"I AM, IN THE NOW!"

You're more than able if YOU allow yourself to be.
It's only impossible when you don't allow Possibility to
mentor YOU! YOU can do anything if you're willing to
learn everything YOU need to accomplish it! ~ The 365

I AM getting more and more comfortable in not only BEING, but in BEING RELEVANT. My mind is becoming more settled in positive Self-worth. Worth can be negative or positive. Wealthy or impoverished. Great or less. Many view their Worth as something irrelevant or irresponsible. The worth of a thing is seen in "the price of the thing!" When we have yet to recognize our Worth "we will price ourselves all over the place!" The price will determine IF others "see our worth of being!"

When we desire to be accepted, if our minds have not yet become full of truth, we will "establish an affordable price" so others can "purchase our acceptance!" I MATTER. I MATTER to ME!

Do YOU matter to YOU? I think I felt ashamed because my need for others "reflected my matter-less existence to myself!" It showed that I never really mattered to myself.

If you have no place to BE in your life, you will simply" be everywhere!" When you are "scattered" you are not obligated to be "in charge or in power!" Excuses come naturally to those who are not living in Power or in Charge. You will naturally employ the "power of excuse" when YOU have not determined where YOU should be! If YOU feel that YOU do not matter, YOU will not BE.

I'm serious! Think about this for a moment. If I feel that I do not matter, I will not BE. I can expect YOU to help me feel better, but my life isn't wired or designed to "awaken" to the voice or opinion of another. My LIFE is only required, wired, and designed to "heed" to the Voice of the Divine within ME! Your LIFE will listen to YOU.

Living to matter to yourself can be a very hard thing when "YOU have put YOU off for so long." Living comfortably and boldly, while "causing others to take notice of your existence," can be mentally disturbing to the life YOU once had by "disguising yourself with the background of humanity!" YOU cannot hide and matter at the same time! YOU cannot lead the way when you're hiding within the "darkness of obscurity and fear!" Excuses will arise when "the fear of being seen" appears!

Are YOU listening to YOU?

: : A LIVING LAW: :

I knew that IF this transformation was going be "validated by me," I would have to pass the test of BEING SEEN and OBSERVED by others, as well as critiqued by their opinion and experience. I had to "face" the fears that once made me doubt myself. We critiqued things all the time, if we are free to admit it. My thoughts, ways, and appearance, was now on display. I knew that there would be others who wanted to see if I "looked the part" of the Image that I captured not only emotionally, but spiritually. I believe the Test was not really from "another," but from myself. It was easy to be in authority by yourself. But how would another person "allow YOU to think that way of yourself, to yourself, and for yourself?" I had to move away from those who would allow me to "play" leader all by myself, which was their way of giving me support! NOW, the TIME had arrived for me to be proven, critiqued, and questioned by strangers in authority. I had to "become what I was speaking!" I had to "earn the right to speak!" During this process, the criticism will be very, very, intense. The Atmosphere has to see if YOU have "earned the right to speak!" It has nothing to do with "being fair!" I had to validate my own discoveries. I had to become my first student, as well as my first graduate! I had to defeat every excuse known to man "in order to be trusted by the Spirit of Wisdom!" There are some things that you can read and remember. And then, there are some things that only few are willing to BECOME! When YOU become a thing, YOU will never lose it. This is a fear that YOU must overcome. How quickly can it be overcame, you ask?

As soon as YOU begin to "love" being criticized...

INNER-LAW #13

I AM ON MY WAY!

---

*When a Defining Moment comes along, YOU define
the Moment, or The Moment will define YOU!*
~ Kevin Costner

I have found that when something **is truly "greater"** in my life, every other altern**ative, or opt**ion, becomes irrelevant on its own. **When someth**ing has become irrelevant, there is no **need to gran**t it any more energy or concern. Distra**ctions becom**e a thing of the past simply because the**re is no positi**ve energy being given to it.

I AM on my way to LIFE. I AM in **my zone. I** AM no longer granting permission to **the illusions** of the mind. I AM on my way to LIF**E!**

Even while I'm moving about in **life, "my m**ind is quiet enough to hear constant **requests that** are being sent to me from my **Journey and Path**!" There is a way to possess a quiet s**pirit, even wh**ile moving about. There is a way to ha**ve an inner q**uiet time, even when the rest of the wo**rld is "speak**ing loudly!"

I have embraced the fact that my **world "is with**in" and not "without!" My world **is ME and** not the bustling routine of the consta**nt ramblings** of human events! My MIND is quiet. It's important to me. Whatever is great in my life will naturally carry influence within it. It will naturally establish what is important, and it will also dictate the priority of importance in my life. It will protect me from excuses.

Whatever I AM loving is creating the way for my life. My Love creates My Way! My WAY creates my fulfillment. I cannot be distracted because I AM in love with my WAYS. My ways reveal within me "The Truth and the Light!" Light prepares a rhythm for me to "see" through the darkness of the unfamiliar! I AM not afraid.

LOVE is a powerful Light that arises at the very appearance of our "soul's connection!" It is so much more than a feeling. It is the Appearance of the Soul's intimate friend!

LOVE for a thing will create the maintaining of that particular thing. LOVE frees me from the distractions of obligation. When I AM afraid to give

myself to the Power of LOVE, I will find myself
agreeing with Distractions, "while giving a constant
Excuse for the obligation!" When LOVE is present,
the fear to be in agreement will no longer find itself
living in me.

I AM on my Way.

:: A LIVING LAW: :

I can't teach YOU how to do it. YOU have to let
yourself do it. YOU have to allow your MIND to
"BE the LIGHT" that it has always known itself to
BE, even when YOU feared it being so. I allowed
the LIGHT to BE whatever it desired to be,
without questioning it, or resisting it! It taught me
what a class could not, simply because The Teacher
"was hidden within the confines of my allowance
and my gift of non-resistance!" I let the Teacher
appear within me and to me. I had to overcome
the labels of "right and wrong." I allowed myself to
"feel the experience" of the Shift. I had no desire

to learn the rhetoric of the Shift. I had to give my life to the reality of the burn. I had to let myself become the "sacrificial lamb" to The Experience. When YOU are afraid of The Way, another "way" will continually invite YOU over to play!

INNER-LAW #14

"I CAN WALK ON WATER!"

Imagine fulfillment until it makes YOU laugh on the inside. Imagine bringing healing to another "till it makes YOU tingle with Pleasure!" The Atmosphere will "tilt" because of it and bring this Opportunity to your Life!

~ The 365

There's this invincibility within **my heart t**hat will not allow me to view **myself as** "an insignificant backdrop in the Universe!" **Th**ere's this inward feeling that permits **me to be a r**uler in the earth. I actually feel that I **can say anyth**ing and it will happen! It may not h**appen today,** but it is Happening. It is stirring in th**e Universe** and within my Inner-Verse. The whee**ls of Power** are constantly turning within me and **I can feel it!**

My thoughts are potent. I can a**ctually think** of something as minor as a television **show that** last aired when I was a child, and beh**old, "there it** is on television!" I can think of a pas**t tragedy in** the world, and behold, "there it is on t**elevision!" I** can think of spreading goodness to a **person whom** I have not spoken to in years, and **behold, "they**'re calling me on the phone, or sendi**ng me an em**ail." Or better yet, sending me a Facebo**ok invite!**

When we live as The Path, all of o**ur goodness** and pleasures come alive, especially w**hen they are** in a blessing mood! I have found o**ut how possi**ble

I really am. I can walk on water. I can walk on the possibilities of seemingly impossible things. Goodness and Love really do desire to be on my side. Love actually loves me. I used to feel ashamed in being loved and embraced. I felt that Love would soon pull the rug from under me and "let me have it!" I felt that it would tell me that it was merely "toying with me" for years while watching me slowly "embrace a significance" that I didn't deserve.

When we feel that we do not deserve goodness, we will hold our inner power, and true identity, "hostage to the darkness of a prison called fear and shame!" We will never allow ourselves to come out and play in the Light. We will find solace "in the darkness," and call this dastardly thing by the name of "peace," and "just being Me!"

When we allow ourselves to come out and play, we will live differently than we've ever imagined. Many of us are outside physically, while hiding on the inside, spiritually and emotionally. There is a Power that arises when we finally "walk out of the Door" that resides within. There's a vibration that occurs within us, taking over our language and spirit. It confirms that we are the offspring of God!

: : A LIVING LAW : :

Oh yes. I suffered from an "inferiority complex," as well as deficient self-esteem. When YOU are afraid of being "all of YOU," Depression will be "all of it," within YOU! After I "woke up," I allowed the Light to shift my mind, as well as how I felt my appearance meant to the rest of the world!" I began to "see" how LIFE responded to me being in it. I began to experience Power and Attraction, both physically and spiritually. Maybe, just maybe, the world was already doing its thing, "and I just suddenly got in tune with it!" I began to feel important, significant, and respected within my own soul. I felt that I was a contributor to the Universe now. It was quite liberating, daring, and different. There are a lot of emotions and possibilities that are lying dormant within us all, but we fear the "interrupters" that are responsible for waking us up out of sleep. Do we feel that this is too much power to have, or better yet, ask for? We can defeat excuses, distractions, and fear, once and for all if we simply desired to. These "evils" will continue to pay the mortgage to live within us "when we fear having a life outside of their usage!" When we are already in bondage and fear within our own mind, we will fear the power to actually fly in the air, and walk on water!

Go ahead and give yourself an entire month of living liberated, thinking liberated, and speaking from a liberated mind. Commit your time to a Responsibility that YOU once ran away from. When reading books, look up the definition of certain words and practice those findings for the month. Try changing your personal schedule also. Refrain from your usual "circle of friends, family members, and associates, who've never placed demands on your potential." Begin to gauge and evaluate your conversations for the entire month. YOU will begin to see the nature of things that you've been attracting all month. Maybe, your conversations are the reason you've been inviting excuses, fears, and distractions, to your life.

INNER-LAW #15

"ILLEGAL TRESPASSERS!"

The aim of Science is not to open the door to infinite wisdom, but to set a limit to infinite error.

~ Bertoit Brecht

I AM. Anything can happen. I AM. It doesn't matter what happens. I AM settled in ME. I AM. When **YOU ARE**, *"the elements will conform to its perception of YOU."* Elements will shift from the energy of your truth. I AM, to the point I am free "to let be!" I AM free to let everything "be" what it is to be. Elements do not change ME. They work with me.

My dreams transcend the ingredients of the elements around me. The elements are not responsible for my dreams, I AM. *I AM responsible within myself. There is nothing hindering me from being true.* I AM true. This Path simply *"enlightened my soul to what was already resident within me, even though I was afraid to see it!"*

I feared being whole. I feared BEING! I needed the elements to advise me and correct me. I needed the elements to hold my hand in fear. NOW, I AM free to BE me, regardless of how the Atmosphere is acting. This is the true Power of the Divine Self. I can remove the "sting from the misery of Life!" This is my Path in Christ Consciousness! I can remove the dominant ingredient from the energy, or law, that I feel is "opposing me" in my own mind. Water is not opposing me, per se. But if I desire to walk upon it, *"there is a law that is present within the nature of the water that will not allow me to walk upon it!"* No matter how much I desire to walk upon it, "there is a law" that is preventing me from doing it.

I can, however, "remove the laws of my own mind that once prevented me from BEING who I was created to be!" We can do EVERYTHING we are designed for. What prevents us from being are "laws that are justifiably placed within our Consciousness." When the "rights of Limitation" are respected, our own limitations will win every time. When our minds have concluded that it cannot be done, our bodies will listen with all of the strength it possesses!

The soul will remove every law that loses its justifiable place of existence within us. When you feel that a barrier, or a parameter, has a right to be there, "we will obey it!" Excuses are the mutual agreements between barriers and mindsets. The barriers are naturally positioned while the mind "acknowledges it and acts accordingly!" But what do you think would happen IF you removed the barrier? What do you think would happen IF the barrier lost its "citizenship in your Consciousness?"

Christ Consciousness is gradually realized as a result of "barrier removals" from the soul and spirit. In order for the barrier to be evicted, it must lose its "right of existence and being!" In other words, the barriers cannot be viewed as temporary setbacks, but as illegal trespassers of Life and Mind!

I must continue to move beyond the permissiveness of "temporary," and see things as illegal, IF they are responsible for "allowing me to use its right of existence against my own self!" There are things that are present in this world "that will allow YOU the rights to use their presence against yourself!" Have you ever had a close friend that allowed you to "use them as a reference" when establishing alibis for your wrong doings or excuses? You know,

"Hey man, tell her that I was with you all day!" "Hey girl, tell him that we went to the mall and the movies!" There are some things in your "mind" that will allow YOU to use them for an excuse.

Are YOU ready to live LIFE without the aid of a "liar within your spirit?" As long as YOU depend upon the persuasiveness of "the liar," your amazing life will take its time finding YOU!

: : A LIVING LAW : :

Hey, if your companions are friends of excuses and fears, YOU will soon be the newest member. Your awakened creativity will "attract" to your life, not just new companions, but new Responsibilities that will be housed in your new companions. Remember, if there is true love within YOU for this Path, YOU will give up your rights of Resistance. When we are afraid of "letting go" of what is "irrelevant," we will have paid the "rent" for distractions, excuses, and fear to reside within us for another year or so. We will never learn when Resistance **is present.** Your Path will require YOU to let go of **the extra weight** of irrelevant relationships. It will **have YOU** to define the nature of everything, an**d everyone, t**hat YOU are connected to. This is a pa**inful experie**nce that many will silently resist in hop**es that the** Shift will "forget about it, and go the ot**her way!"**

You can't teach the Shift. You ca**nnot manipul**ate its emotions. You cannot bribe the **Shift. The** Shift has within it the very Laws of C**hange. The** Shift makes no excuses, neither does it **apologize, for** its actions. The Shift will consider yo**ur companio**ns, even when you aren't. And even w**hen YOU wo**n't!

INNER-LAW #16

"LIVE YOUR LAW!"

Whatever it is YOU believe "will cause the best and worst things to be said about YOU!" You cannot receive the best of that belief "unless YOU are willing to endure the worst that others think, or say about YOU, because of that Belief!" YOU become what YOU have Believed!

~The 365

Pay attention. Pay attention. Distractions are illegal in your world. You are not designed to "lose your Path!" Your Path loves YOU. You can do this. All YOU have to do is make ONE DECISION. Make ONE DECISION that will cause the Atmosphere to *"re-adjust its schedule for your Path!"*

Excuses are reflections of "uncommitted decision making!" You must realize that your life is not obligated to be "dismantled" with every "issue or event" that resides in the atmosphere. You're not obligated *(notice that I keep using the word "obligated?")* to address every single thing in your life. Once you embrace the Boldness to establish "that ONE decision of Purpose," every "event" will revolve itself around that Decision. LIFE will "re-adjust itself" to accommodate your steadfastness, and when YOU DECIDE to take time out of Your Flow to "do something different," it will not count against you as a distraction.

Events will revolve themselves around YOUR

TIME ZONE and not the other way around. Excuses come when we "revolve our life and time" around the movements of other people, places, and things. When we have NO PLACE of BEING "we will connect to the rhythms of what lives beyond us!" When YOU live your Decision, things outside of US will follow the patterns of the Rhythms within US!

But YOU must "allow this reality to resonate within YOU at ALL COSTS!" What costs you say? Many will not comprehend your reasoning for establishing this type of LAW in your life. Accept the misunderstanding from others. There are certain "life events" you may not be a part of with others and they may think you're denying them. Accept it. You must create and embrace the LAWS of Excuse-less-ness in your life. **Live by your LAW.** Choose where and when to involve yourself in the rhythm of others. Believe me, *others are choosing when and where to involve themselves in your game as well.*

YOU must overcome the pain of "allowance"

and letting yourself BE the Truth **you really** are. You cannot afford to make the **right decis**ion "sometimes." *Making the right decision "some of the time" is a bad decision "all of the time!"* **You** must overcome the fear and responsibility **of being ahe**ad in Life!

How do YOU feel about this?

Do YOU feel important in your o**wn world** of YOU?

Do YOU feel that the Atmosphere **is listening** to YOU?

When YOU feel important enou**gh to your**self, "YOU will find yourself brea**king out of** an incredible shell of fear and procrast**ination," and** the Light will come. You may experienc**e periodic b**outs of anger, self-doubt, and even dep**ression. Don't** let the symptoms imprison you. When **Change co**mes, "every comfort zone within YOU **will speak lou**dly until YOU change directions!"

: : A LIVING LAW: :

I remember when I was flying up to Philadelphia for a meeting. The airport was packed, and I was anxious to go. I was flying standby at the time, and I was feeling quite privileged. And flying free too! Well, I kept getting "moved out of the rotation," and that wasn't any fun. Then, I started imagining something incredible. What if I could somehow, "shift the Atmosphere" so it would allow me to "move up" on the flight list, while rearranging the previous ticket-holder's schedule to a different purpose, scheme, or even delay, while yet granting them a successful outcome. At the time, I felt that it may have been rather selfish, or even "make-believe, in a perfect world!" But I thought about it again. Can we "shift" the Atmosphere to accommodate a Will, or Purpose, by releasing its relevance to the discretion of The Atmosphere? In other words, I was going to allow the Atmosphere to discern the priority of an individual's "will and intent," and be open to its verdict. My entire insides shuttered at the possibility! Jesus performed many miracles from this Reality. The tax money from a fish comes to mind. Even His influence with the Laws of Nature, Seasons, and Time. His purpose "hired" various aspects of nature to serve His destiny. The fish that swallowed the coins that were used to pay His and Peter's taxes, was purposely "born" at a certain time. I believe that the fish swam and followed Jesus for years, awaiting the time when a fisherman would lean and lose his money bag while contending with his catch. The fish would then "place the coins in its mouth," and wait for the signal from Jesus. I began to see myself in this same manner. When YOU trust a flow, the Flow will also trust in YOU! I began to wonder what type of Discipline must I continually live to have an effect on the Atmosphere like this? What kind of friendship must I develop with TIME and NATURE in order to have influence like this? Did I have this Thought in order for it to let me know of a Greater Power within me? Within US all?

First, I had to accept the fact that The Universe is willing to "re-adjust itself" on my behalf. On behalf of my disciplines that are consistently lived. I had to accept that the Atmosphere has a mentality and an understanding of honor and influence. I had to embrace the absurdity and audacity of such a reality. When YOU seek a LIFE with this kind of treasure, where will the excuses fit?

INNER-LAW #17

LIVING IN THE LIGHT

Once the "what" is decided, the "how" always follows.
We must not make the "how" an excuse for not facing
and accepting the "what!" ~ Pearl S. Buck

I have no need for excuse. I'm doing what I desire to do. I'm living what and how I'm desiring to live. There is no need for an excuse in my world. You cannot lead me to do what I do not have a Joy to do. Everything I'm doing is JOY. I've even established relationships and associations that will not enable me to live with excuses.

The Path is Joy. Fullness of Joy. Freedom is JOY. Freedom to be as wonderful as I desire to be. Being wonderful isn't arrogant; It's peaceful. I was created from the Divine Seed of Wonder. You too, were created from Wonderful. Arrogance is finding comfort in living un-original. It's finding pleasure in living limited, blind, and "sincere." But how can knowingly being "limited, and blind," be sincere? Just a thought.

The Path is amazing. Even my faults are no longer condemning to me. I do not see myself in weakness, but in continual evolution of myself and my spirit. I've accepted my "questionable and unfamiliar areas" of Self. I no longer see myself as evil. That is

JOY. I no longer fear my "darkness." My darkness is not sin. Believe it or not, we all know why we feel a certain way about everything.

We all are familiar with our egos, even when we are trying to "hide" them from ourselves. We all know what Truth is "removing from us and adding to us at the same time." We know of the personal control we are losing when The Path establishes greater demands within us. The Path constantly reveals a Light and a Way to us. It never tells us to "walk in it" personally, but the natural intrigue within the soul will silently "invite" us into The Light. We know when we are moving forward into it or restraining ourselves from it.

Excuses are awakened when we have consistently, as well as silently, established a pattern within us that restrains our soul from The Light. Our intelligence of Self and Spirit are naturally expanded by our constant habitation within The Light. As we abide in The Light, every fiber of our Divine Being is expanded in Discovery and Recovery of our "lost" lifetimes.

Our physical courage and boldness are but mere reflections of our "invisible courage" that is made possible by living in The Light! As we constantly abide as sons of Light, our Wisdom becomes Light. Our ways become Light. Our very lives become Light.

Are YOU afraid of the Light?

:: A LIVING LAW ::

Observe all YOU have read thus far.

Breathe.

See where YOU stand, right now, in this moment. Are there any urges within YOU to doubt? Do YOU feel that it's a joke? Are YOU feeling insignificant? Are YOU feeling as though YOU haven't been given the permission to change reality? Do YOU feel that you're not allowed to change yourself?

INNER-LAW #18

LIVING MY POSITIVES...

We must not allow the clock and the calendar to blind us to the fact that each moment of Life is a miracle and a mystery! ~ H. G. Wells

---

I'm constantly going somewhere in my Vision and Path. I really have no time for anything else. No, I'm not deep. I'm focused. I'm not trying to "maintain positive energy." I'm simply living in my positives. I'm simply resting in my Energy. This is what I've always wanted. I'm no longer trying to be convinced of it, as though there is something else "out there" that's just as incredible. No. I'm living in my Zone, issues and all. Wait a minute, what issues?

I need no one to "give me any more responsibility." I constantly seek to finish and accomplish the standards that are silently revealed to me through Wisdom. Your MIND uncovers "new responsibilities and opportunities" within every moment. This is how we live the excuse-less LIFE. When you heed the voice of Responsibility from the Unseen, it will bless YOU in the Seen World! Many do not master the silent voice of Responsibility. It's easy to do what someone else tells you to do "because you can anticipate a soon coming benefit from them." But what can YOU anticipate from within? What reward will you receive for "obeying your own mind and Divine Intuition?" What do YOU receive from listening to the Voice of God that resonates within the temple of your very own Life and Mind?

Many seek to obey a God through scriptures written by flawed men than the God that resonates within our very own Image and Likeness. There is a Divine Expression of God which occupy the faculties of your Consciousness, Intuition, Remembrance, Hopes, Dreams, and Visions. I had to accept the fact that I'm not a villain and that I'm not wrong for thinking for myself.

I AM constantly going somewhere in my heart. Even when I'm sitting still, "I am visiting many places within my heart!" I'm obeying my heart. I'm obeying my Sight. I'm obeying my Faith. I'm obeying my Divine Essence. I'm obeying my God-ness! I'm obeying what I love.

My Path does not need to write anything down and release it to me. It naturally reveals within ME everything that I should be BEING! Because when I've recognized who I'm BEING, my Doings naturally manifest!

I'm moving forward in the spirit of an eternal YES! The doors are not only opening for me, but they are removing themselves from the hinges. The Universe is constantly awaiting my Presence. This is a reality IF I allow it to be. When I have become one with this Permission, Life will begin to gradually "change" for me. Well, Life is not really "changing" for me. I AM changing, and the LIFE that I "saw" can now be "seen" perfectly to me and for me. The "angry lions" that I once saw in the streets "have all disappeared!"

Have your fears disappeared? We usually "walk those streets" that have no obstacles, nor despairing images, that seek to haunt us so! Has your mind cleared itself of the illusions that seek to zap YOU dry of your power and strength? Excuses are the explanations that we give on behalf of our potential, for allowing "lies to hold us captive!"

Are YOU yet speaking to the "lies?" I think not.

: : A LIVING LAW: :

It will amaze your associates at how "disconnected" YOU are from the negatives of life. Your continual optimism may eventually bore others, and your positive outlooks concerning life may find itself on tired eyes and ears. What many have failed to realize is that you now have an incredible "in-look" on life. It comes with the enlightenment. As YOU see yourself differently, your world will also be seen differently. Begin to listen to yourself now. Begin to evaluate your optimism and hope. See if YOU can notice how well you are feeling, as well as how focused you've become now! Give yourself some new responsibilities. Begin to practice your new elements of thought and creativity. NOW is the time to transcend those safe and short-term goals. Let's expand this reality even further...

MY MIND NEVER SHUTS OFF

Positive feedback makes the strong grow stronger and weak grow weaker. ~ Carl Shapiro

My mind never shuts off. I have no questions about anything and I'm never asking God WHY He does whatever He does. I'm constantly living in this Place called "IS and NOW!" I'm constantly seeing things unfold before my very eyes. I'm steadily receiving answers before there are any questions. Maybe this is the reason that I "have no questions about anything and I'm never asking God WHY He does whatever He does." Don't mean to sound so redundant, but that's just the way it is.

I'm constantly feeling the urge to take bold steps into Self-Acceptance. It's not always about "doing anything new," but about embracing more and more of what you've once considered "illegal" to even consider. I'm accepting myself "but I'm not really saying it with the words of my mouth." I'm steadily being settled in my "Is" and my NOW. I'm not fighting anything with my mind. I'm not trying to figure anything out. I'm not resisting. Maybe this is what this YES is, "not resisting!" I'm simply allowing my inner thoughts to become my personal laws. I'm not evicting any thoughts away from me. I'm no longer afraid of Thought. I know that I'm not evil. I know that I'm not bad. I no longer fear thought or difference. I'm not afraid of what The Path is revealing within me. I'm not afraid.

I can say that I AM as God. I AM, God. I AM the essence of God. Others may feel ashamed of me for speaking such a statement. I use to fear what others would think about this as well. I accepted the fact that I am made in the image and likeness of God. God creates Gods. He re-creates Himself as US, within US! I feel bold thinking and living for myself. I'm not trying to stir up anyone.

Just myself.

The more I evict resistance from my senses, the more Discovery and Recovery I experience. The fear of "seeing" will always keep one "blind," but the eagerness for Sight "will enable one to see through the Light." I'm not afraid to see through the Light! I can handle it. I'm going to keep walking into the Light. I'm feeling really good about this. I'm feeling an acceleration all around me and within me. The more I move forward into the reality of this Acceptance, the more I feel a control that I wasn't used to having in my Life. I'm not going to let it go and drop it on the ground. I'm not going to let it go. I can handle this Light.

Can YOU?

: : A LIVING LAW: :

Declare to yourself, with boldness, the Truth that YOU know is "true," but it may offend another's perspective or belief. Declare to yourself, with boldness, a reality of Love that may be hard for someone else to love, but YOU are in love with it! Declare to yourself, with boldness, a Revelation of Yourself that may not be favorable. Yet, YOU know it's favorable. Begin to boldly declare all of your goodness to yourself, and even your darkness, and evaluate how YOU feel. What is it about the

131

LIGHT that is so easy to comprehend? And what is it about the Light that is not? Declare to yourself, with boldness, the cutting edge truth that resides within YOU, but the world has yet to see it!

MY SACRED SPACE

---

*Don't insult your self-encouragement by preparing
your heart to fail! ~ The 365*

M y life has grown. My spirituality is no longer confined to the hope of God accepting me, hell awaiting me, and the pressures that come with maintaining a certain standard of perfection and sacredness. I've discovered and realized that this DIVINE LIFE that I'm so passionately connected to "is as natural as my breathing!" There is no warfare in this Path. There are no devils in this Path. It's simply me embracing my Original Reality as a Divine Expression. I am a living breath of the Architect of the Universe. I believe "what the Divine believes!"

I wasn't sent to this world to try to "figure out the religious rules that hinder so many!" I am a reflection of God and a Joy of Divine Thought. I have found happiness and power in this reality. When we love something with the fullness of our soul, "our behavior naturally accommodates that love!" Our intelligence accommodates that love. Whatever we are loving "will also share its energy with us!" Love will share its love with us.

When this Comfort and Settled-ness is in your heart, "you will not feel the need to protect your life from the Questions of Life." What are the "Questions of Life" you ask? The Questions are the constant reminders and thought triggers that may "slander" your present state of being by constantly saying to you, *What are YOU going to do?*

"Who are YOU?"

"Why did this happen?"

"Why do YOU think it's going to happen for YOU?"

"Are YOU good enough?"

"They're looking at YOU?"

"Do YOU think you're going to succeed at this?"

"Do YOU have enough time?" "You're too old!"

"You're too young!"

Excuses are defense mechanisms against the "inner slander of Questioning!" No, it's not an outside spiritual force, or some "demon" for that matter; it's how YOU have always felt about YOU. It's your own evaluation and test score that you're competing against! I feel good about living. I feel that my contributions to "my sacred Space" in the Universe are being validated and legitimized by my own actions concerning them. I'm living my thoughts in the world. I am not "robbing" the Universe of its ideas by merely sitting by the wayside and "mimicking the voice of the Spirit!" I am actively living out "the Thought" that inspired The Divine to create me!

I am living out the inspiration that is responsible for my formation. I am living out the Joy that the Creator felt within Himself "when thinking of me!" I AM an Intended Life-Bearer in the Universe. The Creator intended for me to BE, here. NOW!

The Divine is not separate from me, nor is it "different" from me. The DIVINE creates what is Divine.

Do YOU receive this? Do YOU believe this? Does it resonate within your soul?

: : A LIVING LAW: :

Be thankful for the process. Celebrate it. Honor it. Stop resisting it. Let it flow through YOU. Live thankful of it. Allow your Mind to remain open to the Light of this Truth, and allow it to guide YOU through everything. Live calm in order for YOU to listen to what's going on around YOU. Remain open to what your prayers are speaking. YOU already know which way to take.

NO GUILT...

Opportunities are not offered. They must be wrested and worked for. And this calls for perseverance and tenacity, determination and courage. ~ Indira Ghandi

---

No guilt. No condemnation. I finally accepted myself. I've accepted the fact that God isn't mad at me. I've accepted the fact that I'm "not trying to get to heaven and neither am I trying to miss hell!" My life isn't about where I go when I die, but where I can arrive to while I live! I accepted the fact that many may not comprehend what I'm saying. Others may not feel the safety that I feel in this Path. I had to accept the fact that "my feelings" are not created and established for them but for myself. I wasn't created to "be present in a place after death," but to occupy the ever increasing Mind of the Divine. I live in the mind of God, always. I am a thought of God. A continual, physical reflection of His inner mind. I am the Will of God. I am the Imagination of God "in skin form!" I am His expression, both physical and invisible. Everything we build with our hands are the reflections of an invisible thought, created from an invisible desire, designed on a material called "paper" which is an expression of dirt! I finally accepted this fact.

I've accepted the fact that my Creator has no religion;

therefore, His thoughts of ME carry within it no religious burden. I finally accepted this Path. This WAY. There are many who may hear me and ask me, "Where do you think YOU will go when YOU die?" I will gladly say, "I will go where I'm already living NOW!" Your "Life after Death" experience is continually established by your constant "Death before LIFE" reality! I'm constantly living in the Joys of my Path, naturally putting away anything within my thoughts that cannot "endure" the JOY of LIFE! This is where my constant shift in behavior and habits are awakened. I'm not trying to "get anywhere!" Whatever YOU love, your energy will prepare YOU for the continual use of it.

No guilt. No shame. You live for what YOU want. When you want it, IT wants YOU. Baggage and all. I stopped worrying about my baggage. I have treasures in my baggage. The Path has no weight limits that hinder it from soaring. When I have recognized the Heights that I've desired to climb, "I know how to unload whatever is unnecessary from my life!" I know how to let go. You will never "let go" for no reason. There must be something beautifully inspiring that naturally repels the negative from your life. It will never allow negative in its LIGHT. I know how to let go!

: : A LIVING LAW : :

Remain open to forgiveness. Also, forgive yourself. Do this as a form of strength, not shame. Be willing to reset yourself at all times. Refrain from condemning yourself. YOU will not be penalized for being happy and embracing fulfillment. Discipline is not a bad thing. It is a beautiful thing. The Mastery that YOU seek to avoid "will become the distractions that seize YOU later!"

You should be sensing a major release in your Spirit, NOW. There is no need to feel guilty for discovering the Beauty of Who you've always been…

INNER-LAW #22

NOTHING IS IMPOSSIBLE...

"You can have it IF you're willing to be misjudged for it, despised for it, held accountable to it, and questioned about it." ~The 365

Everything that resonates **within Me** is possible. I can say "more than **possible!**"What is discipline? Am I influenced by **how you re**act to me? Do I really need a positi**ve reaction fr**om YOU in order to live my Path? I **know my P**ath, but do I need you to agree with it**? Am I afraid** of being questioned about it? Can I a**nswer all of y**our questions about "my life?" Can I a**nswer all of** MY OWN questions about my life?

I need to settle my own self in ord**er to answer** my own questions. That's all that matter**s. If I can answ**er for me I can answer YOU! I need t**o settle my o**wn self in order to answer my own que**stions. I need** to quiet myself. I don't need to "see**k opportunit**ies" to "prove" what's in my own min**d. Can I shut** up for a minute? What is discipline?

It's possible. Even more than poss**ible. When I** am more influenced and motivated b**y my Path, t**han I am of your reaction, Possibilitie**s become m**ore doable! If I am more moved by **the reaction** of another, than the truth of my Pa**th, then my** life becomes impossible and chaotic.

I don't care what you think. I can't "care" or even consider it. I love this Path. It has made me aware of my rights of LIFE. I have rights. I have permission. Yeah, that's a better word. I have permission "to permit my greatest desires to consume me and my limitations to forget about me!" I have permission to do whatever I want! I once felt very ashamed about having rights, permission, and power. I felt that my feelings didn't matter. I didn't feel that I had the right to even have a feeling.

I can do all things that are required of me.

::A LIVING LAW::

Live as though you're on an assignment. Embrace the fact that every Moment is a miraculous reality, awaiting your permission to create your heart's desire. YOU should be settled within yourself now. LIFE should be flowing much easier now. Begin to live with a YES attitude. Know within yourself, "that every door is available to YOU!" Live confident and with Boldness. Every second is an assignment, as well as an opportunity, to create a new reality for your LIFE. What do YOU need to BE in LIFE? NO-THING, is impossible to YOU.

Maintain this level of power and discipline. YOU are as powerful as "the fear YOU overcome!"

Inner-Law #23

Oneness & From-Ness

Excellence is not an act, but a Habit. The things
You do the most are the things YOU will do best!
~ Marva Collins

I've learned and have accepted. That's the key to learning, acceptance. Acceptance produces an established thought. It's good to have an established thought that is "flexible enough to discern when it's time to progress and evolve" on its own. It's an awesome reality to produce life giving thoughts. It's even greater to produce Thoughts that can also "think for themselves!" A thought that can think for itself "will not create a resistance to growth and change." When your thoughts possess the freedom to grow, you will too!

I see my Thoughts as more than "mind entertainment." I see them as People. I see my thoughts as co-creators in my life. Divine Imagination. Divine servants to my existence. They challenge me. Provoke me. Move me. My thoughts are people and my words are servants to my beautiful reality of life. How do YOU see every member that works within the parameters of your life and existence?

I have learned and accepted the fact that everyone

will not agree with me. They will listen to my words and have an opposing viewpoint to what I think and believe. No one is obligated to believe everything I say. There are those who have differing views or rules of thought who take their difference to a whole new situation. They project hate towards me or even controversial thoughts regarding me. It's possible to differ without creating "walls of indifference!" It's possible to disagree without separating or destroying one another.

I've accepted the fact that many of these principles are treasures "for me" regarding "my" Path. They may not be treasures for YOU. I have learned that my Path is the establisher of a zone within me called "Feelings, Emotion, and Intuition!" My inner-self is established within a certain standard of Divine Oneness. From this place, "my feelings and sensitivity to Light and Logos (words) are birthed." My place of BEING is rooted within the very core of Divine Values that I have allowed myself to reside in.

My discernment, or intuition, is a direct reflection of the LIFE STATE I reside in. As I live "FROM" this Place, I also "travel" in Spirit, Soul, and Time, from this Place. This is where I "see" and understand from. Many of us possess a place called "FROM" that resides within us. It is "from" this Place that we "see and understand!" The Path in which you live "from" will naturally create "your EYE" of Spirit.

This is the ROAD or PATH of your Divine Self. Whenever we speak of "The Path," we do not speak of a religion or denomination that houses within them an agreeable place of culturalistic or theological comprehension. The Path is your residence of ONENESS and FROM-NESS!

My behavior is established "from" wherever I'm one with. My actions are reflections of what is actually happening within me, and through me. My actions are a mirrored revealing of the ACTS that are taking place within my heart.

::A LIVING LAW::

Grant yourself permission to practice your fulfillment this week. Put some money aside, if need be. Go and bless someone. A friend. A stranger. Go somewhere YOU don't normally go. And bless someone. Practice your Power. See yourself as a Solution and an Answer. Follow your First Mind this week. See where it leads YOU. Open your calendar and schedule week of Intuition.

YOUR ACTIONS MUST BE INTENTIONAL...

Distractions aren't always "surprises!" Sometimes, purposely devoting positive energy to things that are of no purpose at all, are distractions. Time gone. ~ The 365

It's imperative for YOU to *"mean everything YOU do!"* Your LIFE must be intentional, not loose! Excuses and Distractions crave the *"loose life!"* Lives that are not firmly fixed on courage, belief, and oneness of Self, will find itself *"wandering toward the homes of every conflict, drama, and tragedy, no matter how simple those issues may be at the time!"*

Everything boils down to how YOU feel about living inside of YOU! Are YOU comfortable within yourself? No one is empowered to "let" you live intentional. This is a reality that YOU must grant yourself. INTENTION is a natural byproduct of your own spiritual firmness and courage.

INTENTION is also a byproduct of our own power. Do we feel that we can "afford" our place in the world? Do we feel that we are "in trouble?" If you look in the dictionary, there are no pictures of trouble. Yes, there is a definition of trouble. But there are no pictures of trouble. Trouble is a perception that is based on the personal perspective of the one beholding the "decision!" When we lack "the wealth of courage" in our own selves, LIFE will appear to be trouble! When we possess the wealth of courage within us, LIFE will be seen as "more than doable!" Our impoverished self-perspective will continually put us at odds with LIFE. Excuses and Distractions will become the "tormentors and sheriffs" to our Destinies, continually seeking us out in order to arrest us for not paying the bills or the "rent" of LIFE!

When we exist in LIFE without control, focus, or inner wealth, we will naturally perceive ourselves in "trouble or hardship!" Are we in poverty within our own consciousness? Poverty is more than a lack of money. It is the lack of discovered purpose and self-significance. Without self-significance, we possess no intention!

Intention will naturally prioritize your LIFE "according to the needs YOU value most!" It will "place everything within YOU" in the "proper order of significance!" When the values of your LIFE have been recognized by your actions, it will awaken the wealth within.

Intentional living will eradicate the need of excuse as well as the constant submission to distraction. Allow yourself to "become wealthy in self-significance!" Allow yourself to become enriched in Spirit. Remember, there is no trouble. Trouble is "created" and established when we "see ourselves inferior" to what we are facing. When we lack power, we lack movement! When we lack hope, we lack momentum! Trouble will disappear "as soon as our Mindset becomes enriched!" When we can afford to see things clearly, without depression or self-doubt, we have awakened our new heart!

: : A LIVING LAW: :

This month, make a schedule of every intention, desire, and blessing that YOU desire to experience for yourself, as well as someone else, and GO DO IT! Maintain a Focus within yourself that will empower YOU, expand YOU, and increase YOU, to do your bidding. And whatever comes up, or appears, that has nothing to do with the sanctity of LIFE, PURPOSE, or LOVE, avoid it. Let's see if YOU can maintain your Inner Truth and LAW! Let's eradicate distractions this month! And beyond.

Let's eradicate trouble. If I possess a $1,000,000., and my $25,000.00 car breaks down, am I in trouble? But, if I only have $5, and my $25,000.00 car breaks down, I may consider that trouble. Let's see if we can maintain a wealthy standard of consciousness this month!

Inner-Law #25

"Positive Procrastination"

Growth is like creativity, it doesn't go along very neat, precise plans. You get clogged highways before YOU figure out a way to open up capacity. You get pollution before you figure out a way to fight it. ~Steve Forbes

I AM not going to fight you. I AM not going to war with you. I AM where I desire to be. There is no need for me to define an enemy for myself. There is nothing out there. There is nothing within me. I AM not going to fight you. I AM not going to struggle with you. There is nothing out there. There is nothing "in here!"

I remember the constant energy spent in just motivating myself to believe that I can at least start, or, that I was worthy to at least possess an idea. No manifestation. No work. No movement. Just simply telling myself "that I can do it!"

I spent countless hours in "positive procrastination," which is a creative way of speaking success without the actual activity, or workings, to success! I was on a spiritual treadmill, "burning calories in the mouth while viewing the same, familiar surroundings of life and mind!" I had to move. I had to see something NEW and DIFFERENT!

So, I AM not going to fight with you anymore

Excuses. I AM not going to war with you. As a matter of fact, I need to refrain from even acknowledging a barrier between my Path and myself. There are no barriers between what I love and who I am. The energy used to "speak positively" to myself should now be given to the building of my Life and Path. I should never allow myself to be constantly distracted by unfulfilling, positive-self-affirmations. Building up my "feelings and emotions," while being absent of discipline and movement, is a negative reality.

What shall I create today? What is it that I desire to build? Have I wasted time in "speaking positive" that I never took the time to devise a strategy or plan? What Solutions have I developed? Which Questions do I feel to answer? What Opportunity am I developing for those who need it? What Opportunity have I developed for myself?

Excuses can be silently disguised in the form of positive procrastination. Speaking good towards yourself, without the power of movement, are simply "beautiful lies!" What do I "see?" What do

YOU "see?"

AM I "my plan of action?" AM I "my war?" AM I being set free from my fear of ME? AM I afraid?

AM I afraid of being an "I AM?"

What will we build? There is nothing there. There is nothing standing between us. I guess there's no more time to talk. I am NOW building this beautiful city of Light and Life that have always resonated within me. I see it. I AM living within it. I AM speaking from it.

: : A LIVING LAW: :

Since YOU are no longer obligated to fulfill the wishes of a Demand that is no longer related to YOU, "follow your unique inspiration, and create a thing of Beauty." This creation will serve as a reminder of your present freedom, power, and incredible mindset. It will also function as a guardian against the subtle invites that are sent by Fears, Distractions, and Excuses. After a while, the invitations will find themselves "getting lost in the mail!" Live your terms, at all cost. Maintain your commitment to Purpose, even if the methods must change. Sometimes, LIFE will call for us to shift our methods while remaining true to our Purpose.

INNER-LAW #26

QUIET YOURSELF
AND LISTEN...

Look carefully then how YOU walk, not as unwise but as wise, making the most of the time, because these Days are evil. ~Ephesians 5:15-16

Your LIFE already knows what to do with YOU. If YOU listen, YOU will hear it "exposing and revealing plans, attitudes, goals, and directions to YOU!" You will hear your Path speaking to YOU plainly and vividly. It easily answers every question that resides within YOU. Your Path isn't obligated to answer the questions of others' misjudging of YOU. It will answer what the Universe has already established within YOU. The Universe will answer to the call of her own children, and not waste its energy on what another has perceived of YOU!

You can hear your Path speaking. I believe that many of us have created a "self portrait of what we perceive is necessary for our own sanity and survival." Our self-portrait has not found itself mutually agreeing with the Path that is naturally speaking within us. It creates stress on the inside of us as we seek to live out our "Self-Portrait" over the natural flowing river of Unlimited Life that already resides within us, as US!

Every one of US are complete with The Path. Every one of us is already complete and full of God. We are already pre-packaged with The Voice of Awareness. Many have tried to "compartmentalize" this Awareness and give it a "name" or a perspective, therefore ruining and perverting its Timing and Perfection.

Listening and honoring your Path "will naturally lead us away from what would have distracted US!" If you innately believe and accept that YOU are prone for distraction, YOU will find yourself "shutting off the Voice of the Path!" When we become too open and attached to the surroundings and noises of what we call "life," YOU will find yourself constantly being drawn into its vortex of movement and energy as it constantly pulls YOU away from The Voice that is naturally wired within your BEING for guidance!

Stress creates excuse. When you're competing for attention between the Self-Portrait and Your Original Self, you will create stress. You're stretching yourself between dimensions and zones and YOU don't have to do that! If YOU take the time to listen, you will find that Your LIFE is already established and your steps have already been ordered.

Because we have not listened to our Path perfectly, whether intentionally or unintentionally, we are finding ourselves having to live a lifestyle of constant toleration "rather than a life of Divine Celebration!" We are having to "settle" for a manageable life rather than enjoy the benefits of a Recovered Life! Psychologically, many have "silently embraced that the struggle is real" instead of seizing the Power to soar beyond the status quo's that seem so legitimate!

I AM moving beyond sight. I hear and see a clear Path within ME. I AM doing it. I AM making it happen. There's nothing outside of me that's powerful enough to conquer me. I AM allowing LIFE to BE SO!

I AM allowing it to BE, NOW!

: : A LIVING LAW: :

As soon as I developed a Trust in myself, I found myself having the Power to submit to my Ideas of Spirit. It's not that we don't trust the Ideas. We are simply not trusting our own "ways, habits, and procrastinations." We know "when we are going to quit a thing!" We know when we are going to make excuses about a thing. We know it as soon as we hear a subject matter that may peak our interest, but after some time, "we seek the loophole that will allow us the wiggle room to exit, without experiencing the guilt of being a quitter!"

So, I want YOU to sit back. Breathe. Listen within. Tell me what YOU hear. Take courage. Articulate your thoughts. Your thoughts are creating a LIFE WAY for YOU. Your inner-rhythms are fully knowledgeable of your next steps. There is something alive in YOU, here, right now, that is already existing there, right now! Within it is a direction that will show YOU how to get THERE, NOW! You already have this ability, but you've consistently ignored it. You usually call it your "first mind!" This "first mind" has the permission, as well as the audacity, to protect YOU from procrastination, and distractions. It protects YOU by giving YOU the incredible power to say, "NO!"

NO.

"RANDOM ACTS OF PURPOSE!"

It's not the hours YOU put in your work that count, it's the work YOU put in your hours. ~ Sam Ewing

My passion and thoughts are the creators of Miracles. There are very unique places that I find myself in. Well, not exactly "find myself in," but you get the drift. My Path establishes a very unique journey for me. When you find yourself living "free" from the need of predictability, your Passion will establish within you "random acts of Purpose!" These "unpredictable" structures of Wisdom are not obligated to find its "daily rhythms through a carefully orchestrated series of events" that are in agreement with your foreknowledge and familiarity! Faith has a way of establishing the Journey in a very powerful way "when we become one with Everything in our world!"

I live this way. And yes, there are "some things" that may arrive as a surprise, but really "I'm not totally surprised!" I may be surprised at the fact of not preparing my world sooner for something I actually "heard" in my spirit earlier. Believe it or not, whether you desire to accept it or not, "we actually hear what's going to happen!" May it be by intuition, feeling, or that "little something that seemingly nudges us" continually.

I allow these Random Acts of Purpose to simply "live its life" through my life. I AM an "intentional act of Divine Thought" that allows "intentional, yet random acts of Purpose" to happen. I possess what I allow to Happen. Our Divine LIFE employs both LIGHT and DARKNESS. The Will of God will create with everything It has established. Whether I know everything or not, it doesn't matter.

My spirit is "kissed by the future happenings" of my life. When I am quiet enough, I can actually feel "the possibilities of my Life establishing themselves through my habits and emotions." The vibes of my future will begin to intertwine themselves in my imagination and thought. My perspectives shift towards the environment and value systems of my "future Reality!" My Destiny is sending invitations to my emotions, awareness, and consciousness, and I begin to "hear" new languages concerning my Path!

You will become it before YOU "see it!" My behavior begins to take on the attitude of where I'm awakening to. You will know "before you know!" Before I see it, "I am BEING IT!" My present surroundings must either expand themselves for ME or evict me from it! I am not being rejected, but ejected into a greater reality! I needed to know the difference between rejection and ejection!

I've gotten to a place where I no longer "make choices" to live this way. I AM living this way. I'm not "up and down" with my life. I AM living my life. I AM not living this life "when the elements allow me to." I AM in spite of the elements. The elements are nothing. I AM living my life. Nothing is allowing me to do it. Whatever is responsible for "letting me" do something worthwhile "is the real master of my life!" If my friends are letting me live my life "then they're my masters!" If my career is letting me live, then my career is my master! You got it.

When YOU are at Peace with your Path, your much

anticipated future will prepare you naturally and spiritually. It will train YOU "through the Moments of TIME and the silence of Thought!" This is the beauty of Imagination. It can do whatever it desires to do. It is the Sovereignty of God, as YOU.

:: A LIVING LAW: :

Strengthen your self-commitment. Celebrate your ideas by allowing them to remain a constant in your life. It takes nothing to produce beautiful ideas; but it takes everything to live them out. By this time, YOU should have gained some trust in yourself, as well as your habits. Your habits will naturally rise to the degree of LOVE you have for a thing. Excuses are always attracted to the beauty of bad habits, while Distractions constantly flirt with the undisciplined. See yourself as important, significant, and necessary. Not just to others, but to yourself as well.

INNER-LAW #28

"SO, WHO AM I SPEAKING TO?"

Your Life will obey whomever **YOU** *do.*

~ The 365

"So, Who Am I Speaking To?"

I AM feeling incredible and responsible. I AM feeling as though I can make a relevant and incredible contribution to the world. I feel that I matter, finally. I had to grant myself permission to matter. I had to grant others their own freedom in perceiving me. I had to grant them their own judgment of me. I had to grant others the same freedom that I desired for them to "allow" me to have. That's it. I thought that others had "power" to give me a freedom that was already owned by me. I didn't realize that what I really wanted was to make decisions, "and silently obligate others to purchase it, buy into it, and invest in it!" I wanted them to own the consequences of my decisions and choices by applauding my decisions and choices. I needed them to say YES to me. I needed them to adore me and love me. I needed them to "make me the Person that I was afraid of making, or even recognizing," for myself! I needed them and was angry because they didn't seem to need "my affirmation" to be anything!

Why are we so afraid? What is it about us that we

deem as shameful? What is it about our look that we despise? How were we able to give so much of ourselves away and not even know about it? How were we able to do that?

I thought that "they" felt that "they" were better than me. I guess it was ME who created the equation, as well as the common denominators that granted me the equation. I created "the standard of excellence" and counted myself out of the Game!

So, WHO AM I SPEAKING TO? Who's listening to ME? Sometimes, we scream so loud just so we can hear OURSELVES. Are we listening to ourselves? Or, are we angry at the fact that we desire others to allow us to borrow their consciousness in order for us to "speak to ourselves through them!" Are we using others to serve as mediums for our own selfish need of recognition? Are we needing to hear ourselves talk through the opinions and acceptance of another?

I AM feeling wonderful. Today...

: : A LIVING LAW : :

I actually expect the Atmosphere to listen to me. I expect it to adhere to my Voice. No, I do not randomly "throw requests" in the air that possess no meaning, nor Universal good. I expect the Flow of the Atmosphere to position me with people, places, and things that will draw out the ultimate best in me, while even subjecting me to the ultimate "cleansing and transitions" that are necessary for my good.

"And we know that God causes everything to work together for the good of those who love Him and are called according to His purpose for them," Romans 8:28 NLV

The Atmosphere, or Rhythm of Things, will mirror my heart, invite the necessary Shifts that are necessary, and prepare me for the Turns, even when I'm ignorant of its plans. So, we must maintain a Mind for change. We must expect Change. We must embrace the reality of being "prepared by the Will of God" for things we may not be planning for on our own. But somewhere in your heart, YOU actually are.

INNER-LAW #29

THE CENTERED SOUL... (THE EXCUSE-LESS LIFE)

So, who's keeping YOU? Is it the fear of Responsibility? Or, the fear of leaving the familiar, and never going back to visit? Sometimes, the answers are more than intimidating than the misery! ~**The 365**

The greater the distraction of the soul, "the harder it is to connect and focus the soul!" Distraction is the inability to maintain a healthy, thriving focus of Soul and Center. It reveals the improbability to maintaining a Divine-inspired balance within the soul.

Distraction comes in many forms. Distraction is more than "a temporary lapse of forgetfulness." Distraction is a "misstep" within the Soul. It hinders the Consciousness from maintaining its natural Divine function of Self-Empowerment, Imagination, and Discernment. It hinders creativity and comprehension. It attracts the excuses that we use to "cover up our lack of commitment and preparation!"

I AM settled. My soul is present with me in all things. My soul is fulfilled in LOVE, WISDOM, and POWER. My soul has identified these things "as its own food supply." I constantly feed my soul every good thing. My soul has no desire to travel apart from my Spirit and my Truth. My soul has no interests in anything that will not empower it to thrive. My soul is settled in goodness, mercy, and power. My soul gives me ideas "of the foods that it desires to become even more powerful." I AM quiet enough to listen to my heart. I AM "my heart!" I AM existing in this LIFE "as many forms and many sounds!" Within me "is everything!" I AM the fullness of God, every day, and in every moment. I AM not an attraction for excuses. My LIFE is enjoying the Path that it's on. I have no place else to exist. I AM in God and God is "as I." God and I "are one." We are the "same!" There is no difference in God, nor, in myself. We exist as ONE. My soul is centered and aligned with Love and Truth.

I AM capable of making decisions that I can co-exist with. My decisions are residents of my "inner house!" Decisions are not strangers. Decisions are the results of my power. Decisions do not visit me. I create them. I nurture them. I am "their Parent!" Decisions are my children. They are created from the seeds of my mind, spirit, and values. Decisions only feel like "strangers" when I AM "being strange to myself and to Purpose." Decisions are good "when I AM good" and disobedient when I AM "disobedient" to my natural course of truth.

If my decisions are distracting me, then "I AM not the ONE making, or creating, the decision." If I live disconnected from I AM, then "Disconnection" is the person making and creating the decisions for my life! A disconnected decision will make me a "disconnected individual!"

And I AM not a "disconnected individual!"

:: A LIVING LAW: :

When I "arrived" to this point of Thought, I was able to identify my "life partners, companions, and associates." I was able to intuitively, develop my CIRCLE of RELATIONSHIPS. My relationships are reflections of my daily emotions, creative hunger, and intentions. Our desires and flows of life are found within the physical presence of those who are constantly with us. Look at those around YOU. Listen to your conversations. Are YOU enjoying them? When the Thoughts are healed, the body glorifies itself within the Power!

I began to only create in life, those things I found worthy to go through, or experience. YOU can determine the degree of "Shifts and Detours" that YOU find exceptional enough to entertain. If YOU desire to entertain it, then YOU will never lose TIME. If it's on your "schedule,' TIME will reserve itself for it.

INNER-LAW #30

THE FAMILY OF ME...

*When your life's hunger is to give the **unlimited good**,
the Divine will remove the hinges from **every door** that
seemingly stood in your way, and will **grant YOU** access
to the entire Universe! ~The **365***

I AM loving what I'm doing with my Life and my Mind. I AM loving the Places that my dreams are introducing to me. I AM also allowing "my humanness to come along for the Journey!" All of the members of my FAMILY OF ME must come along if I AM to experience fulfillment and joy. WHO ARE THE MEMBERS of the FAMILY OF ME, you ask? My thoughts are members of me. My feelings. My emotions. My desires. My perspectives. My creativity. My sensuality and sexuality are members of the FAMILY OF ME. My spirituality. My commitments. My daily regime of beingness and confidence, are all members of the FAMILY of ME.

The boldest thing I CAN accomplish in life is BEING MYSELF. Greatness is the reality of living your originality "in a world that has become copies in order to be accepted or valued in the eyes of another!" I AM loving the career of ME. How about YOU?

Who said that we cannot live the life of Dreams?

I'm not speaking of dreams in the form of mere, material things. Even though "material things" may be a simple benefit of "dream living," we do not live for "stuff!" I AM speaking of existing totally in the world with your mind and spirit in total harmony with, and in, one another. I speak of LIVING in LIFE.

Excuses will always come when you're trying to accomplish something that YOU have no love for! I AM accomplishing everything I love. And if I don't love it "then it's not for me!" I AM committed to live the LIFE I love. Wherever there is love, there is strength. Wherever there is love, there is power. Wherever there is love, there is peace. Wherever there is love, there is consistency. I AM in LOVE. When Love guides our lives "excuses die!" They are irrelevant. We are free of them. They are free of us.

I AM living from LOVE. LOVE is an incredible power to exist from. I AM not living what I have to. I AM living from what I AM loving constantly. Excuses arrive when I AM doing "what I have no need of." If I AM desiring "acceptance" from something I HAVE NO NEED OF, "then I AM NOT loving myself in fullness!" I AM not going to attract to me those things I HAVE NO NEED OF!

My FAMILY would not appreciate that...

: : A LIVING LAW: :

Outside of your family, begin to identify the loves of your LIFE. Begin to determine those things YOU would love to see yourself doing every day of the week. Begin to identify the experiences YOU would love to manifest in your life. Allow yourself to "see" your Passion of Spirit. Do YOU trust yourself enough to "live your daily life" through them? Or, have you separated this "pleasure" from your domestic life? I personally developed a daily life from my Passion. I didn't evict discipline from my Passion. When we evict discipline, we create a fantasy called "vacation!" But when we allow the Power of Discipline to remain within the cores

of our Passion, we will discover a thing called,
PURPOSE!

INNER-LAW #31

THE PATH OF EXCUSE-LESSNESS!

LIFE responds, not according to what YOU say, but according to who YOU feel YOU truly are! ~ The 365

How excuse-less, not sinless, are you becoming as you evolve into a greater sense of your Divine Self? The more excuse-less you become, the more intentional YOU are living. The more you become your DIVINE SELF, the more you no longer fear "the light or darkness, the unfamiliar or the questionable concerning you." You no longer see a dark road as bad, simply for the fact that a road, with no light, can still take you to your desired destination! You no longer equate the difference between LIGHT and DARKNESS as "good and evil," or "heaven and hell." You simply see it as "the unknown or the unfamiliar!" Your fear of sin is eradicating, or has eradicated.

You've realized that The PATH may be lighted in various seasons of your evolution, or even encased with darkness in another season. As you've evolved, you yet see The PATH has necessary, significant, and empowering. Beloved, this is a treasure that is so beautiful and empowering to find within YOU. It is a new dimension to comfortably "see" this for yourself, by yourself, and through yourself. How real have YOU become? Are you comfortable in what YOU see in YOU?

Are you afraid to change course? Direction? Have you determined when it is time to Shift? Jump? Run? Or, sit still? Are YOU comfortable in your Path? How comfortable have you become with Darkness? Do you still see it as "evil?"

You will get to a point where YOU do not have to "know everything" within the confines of your senses and humanness. There is "this thing" within YOU that already knows. Have you quieted yourself enough to make sense of it? Try to articulate it. Say it to yourself before YOU say it to another.

When you have embraced yourself, "the excuses that naturally stir themselves to being, will soon find themselves dying," simply for the fact that you no longer feel that you must defend yourself for being alive. When you feel the need to defend your position for any reason, you will employ the "weakness of excuse!"

So, are you comfortable in your PATH?

: : A LIVING LAW: :

I validated myself. Therefore, I have no condemnation, neither do I have a subtle need to be "qualified, or approved, by another!" Only YOU will know when this "shift" has occurred within. When your validation has "passed the requirements and standards" of your own soul, YOU will find that the Distractions that so easily beset YOU, are gone. I realized that excuses and distractions were in my life simply because I was using them. I needed them. LIFE will give YOU what YOU need, whether it's good or bad. Have You validated yourself? Has your "Self" found honor in YOU? Has your "SELF" found You interesting, influential, and respected? Has your "SELF" found trust in YOU? Are YOU putting your "SELF" at peace? Find the trust in YOU. Refrain from doing things that will leave a bitter taste to your own Mind. Refrain from doing things with no purpose. Refrain from creating "mind memories" and "triggers" that will contradict your Purpose. When YOU feed "bad food" to your soul, she will "tell on YOU" when YOU seek to do something good for YOU! Feed your soul the same food that feeds the Pictures you are seeing in your mind.

THE SPIRITUAL AND THE PHYSICAL...

YOU will constantly attract what you're constantly
ready to do! Those who win, will attract opportunities
that maximize. Those who employ excuse will attract
"obligations that will justify the need for excuse!"
~ *The 365*

When I speak to my situation, "I desire not only spiritual results, but physical results!" I desire the same, tangible connectivity, even greater, than the tangible expression that I experienced as a result of the circumstance. If the issue has touched me "in physical form," effectiveness would also be created in "physical forms!"

My disciplines should reflect the nature of the atmospheres that I seek to co-create with. My disciplines should possess within them "the same dynamics and ingredients" as my goals. Within my positive thoughts, feelings, and words, should also be the implementation of my physical activities and connectives. My MIND and BODY are teammates, not enemies.

It is totally possible to gain power over the "world of excuses" when our lifestyles transcend the "need for the use of excuses!" When our physical habits have not shifted, as our "mental thought," we will steadily create "physical hindrances for ourselves" that can become "too tiring to overcome!" We may know the right things "and still become hostage to a physical prison of bad habits and non-execution!"

Excuses are created, naturally and creatively, from the "permission and authority" established by "unhealthy and inconsistent" habits of life and mind. Your imagination may say "YES," but your habits may say "NO" to every blessing that resides within YOU! My natural world is established from the mastery of my spiritual world. Your spiritual world is not a religion. It is the essence of the Values that are responsible for your perspective on life as well as your own existence!

How YOU feel about yourself will "establish a habit, or rhythm, within YOU!" It will create a "beat" or "tempo" within YOU. It will determine how YOU react to responsibility, whether initiated by YOU or "someone else!" Have YOU determined "the pace" you're on right now? Excuses are created when we are ignorant of "the tempo" that's been established by the Responsibilities that are seeking to get our attention in life and spirit. Are we ready to embrace this mastery and control? Is there something else "pulling on us" that is draining us of focus? Do we actually feel that this type of Focus is "beyond reality?"

So, can YOU describe the "SEED" that is creating your HABITS and RESPONSE-ABILITY?

: : A LIVING LAW: :

Habits are the "muscle memory of your Experiences." They serve as the "cookies and history" of your Life History, just as the cookies on your personal computer serve as the "history tracker" of your online visits. As I opened myself to the demands and responsibilities of my Passion, I found that it would not allow me to flow in harmony with the comfortable habits and personalities that I'd acquired in life. Your Intention will naturally create contention between YOU and your "muscle memory of experience!" This contention will determine if you're ready to shift!

No resistance.

Don't make a temporary change out of a long-term Reality. Don't "cheat" the Process!

What Am I Going to Lose?

You are only as amazing as the worthiness YOU feel within yourself! Struggles are the natural results of feeling unworthy, even when the unworthiness is "resting silently!" ~ The 365

I am related to God in every sense of the word. It just IS, no need to explain. I feel that I cannot be lost, thrown away, or evicted from The House. I am more than "one of His children." Maybe you feel that I'm taking this "God thing" for granted. I can assure you that I'm not. And I don't feel that you need reassuring of that. You are an offspring of God yourself. There is no need to convince you of my thoughts, or even my Path. I'm comfortable in being a living reflection of the Divine.

Excuses and Distractions are welcomed "weaponry" in the defense of being fearful and ignorant to one's own life and way. When YOU know who YOU are and why, the need for acceptance for your convictions are no longer necessary. There's no need to defend what You so naturally own. I own my life. I own my Time. I no longer need to share my time to gain acceptance. I can say NO to whomever I need to say NO to. I can say YES wherever a YES is necessary. I am not going to lose ME. I am not going to allow ME to die for anything or anyone. Don't you know how hard I fought for "the right to no longer fight?"

I found myself.

I was already here, but I couldn't see it. I couldn't see myself for looking at others. I found myself within myself. I was so ashamed of myself that I closed myself to myself. I actually hid myself from myself.

This is a wonderful feeling. I cannot be lost. How can I be lost when my Father owns everything? When you own the world, every Place is HOME! How can I be lost, when everywhere I journey to, is HOME? Say this with me, *"I OWN EVERYTHING!"*

I have no room to make excuses. What am I going to lose for saying NO to YOU? Your friendship? Your acceptance? Are you going to be mad at me for saying NO? Are you going to hate me, despise me, or reject me, for saying YES to myself? Will you despise me for loving myself, freeing myself, and embracing myself, *AGAINST YOUR WILL?*

Is this how "this" relationship is supposed to be? I broke free from fear a long time ago.

I am not willing to return to it…

: : A LIVING LAW: :

Allow the pure, unfiltered essence of Love, and everything it represents, to celebrate YOU right now, in your soul. Allow the goodness of Peace to bless YOU, right now. Allow the Language of God to speak beautiful things over your life, right now. Let the Peace of God speak well of YOU, right now. Allow your Imagination to overtake YOU, right now. Allow yourself to BE the Perfection you so easily feared. Allow yourself to experience Perfect Peace, right now. Allow yourself to BE the most beautiful person in the world, right now.

Set TIME aside to Bless everything within YOU!

Inner-Law #34

"What are YOU Listening For?"

A Life Solution, that arrives unexpectedly, has a way of awakening the hidden excuse in YOU if you're not careful. The Visionary must also condition themselves to expect an encounter with NOW! ~*The 365*

You have what you're listening for. What do you "listen for?" What are your ears "tuning in to see?" What is the information YOU can live without? We attract what we're constantly listening for. If I'm not listening for it, I cannot listen "to it!" If I'm not listening "to it" then it's "NOT HERE!" If fear is here then I'm listening to it. I'm listening to it because I was listening "for it!" Wealth isn't here "if" I'm not listening to it by way of discipline, power, and habit. If I'm not listening to it "then I wasn't listening FOR IT!" I can't attract it if I'm not listening "for it!"

Whatever "comes to YOU" in life simply answered the invitation that was sent from your Soul. Whatever it is that you're listening for "will dictate a letter in spirit, and inquire of a search party" to "find and recover" whatever that thing is that you're meditating on, regardless of the quality of what you seek!

The soul constantly resonates within a vibe of hope and pursuit. It's constantly "pulling into your life" everything you feel "you're supposed to experience, regardless if it's good, bad, or questionable!" If YOU feel that YOU deserve it, "you'll reserve it!"

YOU are a tuning magnet for every source of energy in the Atmosphere. What YOU "feel obligated to entertain" will break every barrier around it in order to get to YOU! Remember, YOU determine who the visitors and residents will be in your "HOME!" If YOU feel obligated to host "drama, chaos, and disorganization," THEY WILL COME! If YOU feel the need to host "peace, togetherness, and unlimited-ness," THEY TOO, WILL COME!

Listen, "shifts in life will happen," sometimes beyond our control. But YOU can determine how a Shift "will shift YOU," if YOU must be shifted! YOU can determine the priorities, the magnitude, and the effectiveness of the Shift "simply by constantly tuning into the Greater Things of Spirit!"

When I "listen for the Greater Things of Spirit," the Greater Thing will share its Thoughts with ME.

It will transfer its energy to ME! It will transfer its "directions to ME!" The Greater Thing will make ME a "Great Thing" as well. I BECOME WHAT I LISTEN FOR! I BECOME WHAT I LISTEN TO!

I'm constantly "listening for Opening Spaces, Opportunities to Create, and New Transformational Environments!" I'm constantly listening for these Places within others also. I'm listening "for" it by listening "to" it!

: : A LIVING LAW : :

Allow your LIFE to love YOU!

And don't forget to say, "Thank YOU!" Often.

I love YOU.

Thank YOU.

There's no excuse, distraction, or fear alive, that should hinder YOU from the POWER of LOVE.

Until next TIME...

About The Author

Undrai Fizer enjoys life as an author, teacher, and accomplished jazz pianist, creating the original genre of "consciousness" music.

Not only is he a practitioner of divine principle and life, he is also the founder and CEO of Kairos Inter-Global, a module formulated to provoke and inspire thoughts that lead to personal and spiritual enlightenment, purpose, and awakening. He shares his life with Bridget E. Fizer and their three sons Benjamin, Loren, and Zion in the city of Houston, Texas.

CPSIA information can be obtained
at www.ICGtesting.com
Printed in the USA
FSHW021448050519
57860FS

9 780578 168333